BARKERVILLE DAYS

Caitlin Press Inc.
3375 Ponderosa Way
Qualicum Beach, BC V9K 2J8
www.caitlin-press.com

Cover design by Vici Johnstone
Front cover image C-09298 courtesy of the Royal BC Museum and Archives
Printed in Canada

Caitlin Press Inc. acknowledges financial support from the Government of Canada and the Canada Council for the Arts, and the Province of British Columbia through the British Columbia Arts Council and the Book Publisher's Tax Credit.

Library and Archives Canada Cataloguing in Publication

Title: Barkerville days / Fred Ludditt ; with new introduction by Karin Ludditt.

Names: Ludditt, Fred W., author.

Description: Includes index. | Originally published: Vancouver: Mitchell Press, 1969.

Identifiers: Canadiana 20220214220 | ISBN 9781773860954 (softcover)

Subjects: LCSH: Barkerville (B.C.)—History. | LCSH: Gold mines and mining—British Columbia—Cariboo

Regional District—History.

Classification: LCC F5799.B3 L83 2022 | DDC 917.11/7504—dc23

BARKERVILLE DAYS

Fred W. Ludditt

CAITLIN PRESS
Qualicum Beach, BC

Publisher's Note

Having been written in the 1960s, Fred Ludditt's *Barkerville Days* reflects ideas of the nineteenth century, and it contains now obsolete ideas of settler colonial "pioneers." We have chosen to alter the original text in places where a word or term, though descriptive in the last century, is now considered offensive. Such wording has been changed to reflect current and more respectful language. The publisher wishes to acknowledge that Barkerville sits on the ancestral and unceded territories of the Dakelh and Secwépemc Peoples.

To the
Barkerville pioneers

CONTENTS

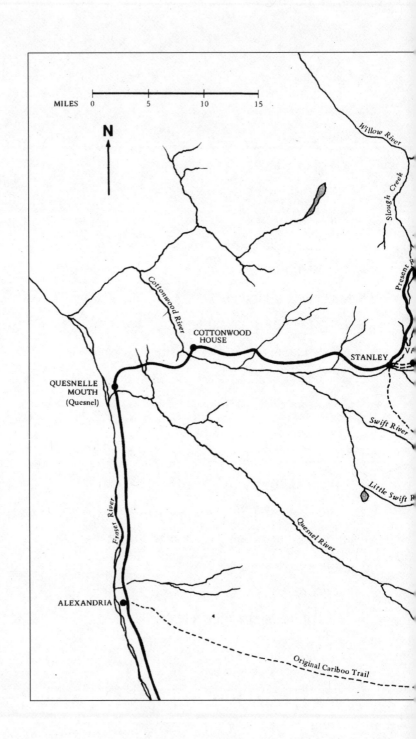

Windlass at the Barker Claim, Williams Creek; also known as the "Never Sweat Claim." Image A-03858 Courtesy of the Royal BC Museum and Archives

FOREWORD

I first met Fred Ludditt, the author of this book, in the old gold town of Barkerville during 1935. The world was caught in the grip of the Great Depression at that time. Living conditions were tough for working people everywhere, but Barkerville was one of the few bright spots. With a new quartz discovery at nearby Wells, and with the price of gold doubled from $16 to something like $32 an ounce, the district was very active. There were three thousand and more people in the Barkerville area during the early 1930s, while only a few years previously scarcely a hundred people lived there. Everywhere there was activity. Men were discovering new gold deposits and rediscovering old ones that could be worked profitably because of the higher price of gold.

Fred and I met in this atmosphere of seeking and searching. While I held a job operating one of the general stores, Fred was engaged in every phase of mining activity. He delved into hard-rock, underground work, placer mining, claim staking and various exploration ventures. He has held claims in his beloved Cariboo continuously since the year 1935 and retains a keen interest in all that happens in the Barkerville region. His final activity there was holding the position of Government Sub-agent at Wells, which he relinquished in 1963.

Yet the search for the gold itself was never enough for Fred Ludditt. The complete drama of the Cariboo caught him early and has since held him fast. Warm-hearted and intensely interested in people, he sought the human stories behind the mounds of washed rocks, the tunnels, the shafts and drifts, and the piles of tailings which are characteristic of any gold mining country.

Fred Ludditt was fascinated by the men and women whose travail had caused the man-made canyons and the massive scars on the face of the land. He was fascinated by overgrown mountain trails and followed them to their end. Then, with eager curiosity, he would ask old-timers about his new find, and so add to his knowledge of Cariboo lore.

It has often been my privilege to tramp over mountain trails with the author. Picking our way up distant creek beds, we have gazed in wonder together at the almost forgotten ghost towns on Grouse and other creeks. In many Cariboo cabins we have talked late into the night, beating back the cold of winter with the warmth of close companionship.

Not only did Fred amass hundreds of anecdotes as he talked with old-timers in his ceaseless search for authentic information, he also read all available written material about the sprawling land we call the Cariboo. He delved into the archives, wrote countless letters and spoke personally to nearly every living person mentioned in this book. All this added together makes *Barkerville Days* authentic. The strange and fascinating story of Barkerville and the Cariboo comes through with a new freshness from every page. It is obvious that few men could be so suited, both by temperament and ability, to tell its story.

In *Barkerville Days* Fred Ludditt comes through as a kindly and sincere man who tells the story of his beloved Cariboo superbly.

Bill Ward
Fish & Game Branch
Victoria, BC

MY BARKERVILLE DAYS

I can still, to this day, hear the *clickity-clack* of my mom's typewriter as she worked on my dad's book—this book, *Barkerville Days*. My father had placer mined around Barkerville in the 1930s. After the Second World War, he brought his bride, Esther, to the Barkerville area where they built a log cabin and sluiced the gold-bearing creeks during the summer and fall for a few years.

But by the time my brother and I came along, our family lived in the "big house" on the only street in Barkerville. All the homes faced the one (nameless) street (there was also a back lane). At that time, Barkerville boasted a population of about one hundred people. I have fond memories of growing up in Barkerville, hauling water and wood, even as a small child. My brother, Frankie, and I were the only two children living year-round in the town until 1958 when we were moved to the nearby gold-mining village of Wells. We had to move from our hometown so that it could be turned into a "tourist trap" by the government of BC. At least, that's how I felt about it then.

I don't really know how long it took my dad to write *Barkerville Days*, but as a child it seemed to me to take forever. My parents, constantly poring over photos sent by my father's friends and colleagues, had little time for us kids. We played outside over by Williams Creek (named after William "Billy" Barker) with our dog Toby.

My mother's typewriter was a big black thing with round keys that sat at one edge of our large wooden table. Beside it were the completed sheets of paper. Piles and piles of paper. It fascinated me to watch her push the carriage return and hear the *ding*! She used carbon paper to keep a rough copy for herself. The room they worked in was heated with a huge barrel-drum furnace, and at night the cat and dog would lie under it and burn the ends of their whiskers.

Our living quarters and bedrooms were upstairs, and this heater sent its warmth above. We did have a small electric heater up there as well, beside which my mom had her homemade wine bubbling in a wooden cask. I was just tall enough to peer inside it and watch the grapes fermenting away. My bedroom faced the street, and at night

Fred Ludditt with his daughter Karin, and son, Frank, in front of their home in Barkerville, 1957. Photo Esther Ludditt

I could see Mr. Dowsett reach up with his long pole to twist the streetlamps on at dusk. In the mornings he would be there again, when the sun came over the mountains, to twist the lights off.

I remember being entrusted to help sell my dad's first pamphlet, entitled *Gold in the Cariboo*, during the summer months, long before Barkerville became a Historic Site. My mom would set up our green card table in front of St. Saviour's Church, put two chairs there for Frankie and me, give us a pile of pamphlets and a float and tell us to sell as many as possible to the odd tourist who happened to either drive or walk through the town. The pamphlets sold for fifty cents each.

Meanwhile, my parents would be working on *Barkerville Days*. During my years in Barkerville my father's employment varied. At first he had a gold mine up at Grouse Creek. After my mom convinced Dad to stop placer mining, the bottom half of the big house became a small store; I believe it might have been called The Trading Post. That didn't last long, and the bottom half of the house became the Government Agent office. When in 1958 we moved to Wells, the office came with us. My father was furious about this because if the Government Agent's office had remained in Barkerville, it would have celebrated one hundred years there. It did amaze me to see my dad so worked up about this, as he was the most even-tempered person; he smiled a lot and always looked on the bright side.

The creation of the book continued, my dad writing and my mom deciphering his handwriting and typing up page after page. We were in Wells until I was about twelve, then we moved to Comox. But it took years for the book to be edited; all the "political stuff" my dad had written had to be cut out. The original version of the book contained many more stories about the old-timers and other interesting people; these were also removed but later published as *Campfire Sketches*. *Barkerville Days* was finally published by Mitchell Press in 1969, the year I graduated from high school.

Today, after paying a few visits back to Barkerville—notably for the fiftieth anniversary of its founding as a Provincial Heritage Site—I have been asked by many who are interested in keeping this history alive to reprint my father's book. Thank you to Vici Johnstone and her team at Caitlin Press for making this happen.

Karin Ludditt
Vancouver, BC
Spring 2022

1
THE KINDLING OF AN INTEREST

The first time I saw Barkerville, in June 1930, I had no idea it would become for me a place of infinite interest and that here I would store up memories to last a lifetime. A friend and I had come up from Quesnel for a visit, but though we had heard a great deal of this old mining town we were on that first day rather disappointed. Barkerville lies in a very narrow valley, with a steep hill which leads to Barkerville Mountain on the right as you enter, with Williams Creek and another hill on its left. The hours of sunshine are short, the hills making for an early sunset and late sunrise. There is one long, gravelled street, a continuation of the road into the town, and one back lane. As we walked up the street, we saw patches of snow against some of the buildings; and a chilly breeze was blowing from a narrow ravine at the upper end. We were pleased at the prospect of leaving it the next day.

However, on returning to Quesnel, where I'd been mining for gold on the Fraser River, I began to think more and more of gold in the Barkerville area. The gold on the Fraser is very fine and so light that at times it seems a puff of wind will blow it away. I knew the coarse, heavy, Cariboo gold could not be found here and so I began to make a thorough study of the old mining records and reports of the district with the idea of going to Barkerville to prospect. It was from the study of those old records that I became more fully aware of the tremendous contribution Barkerville and the surrounding area had made to the history of British Columbia. As I read of the early prospectors and their amazing discoveries, my enthusiasm grew, and I dreamed of walking along the same trails they had taken seventy years before and of finding my own Eldorado. The Grouse Creek area, five miles from Barkerville, appealed to me particularly and seemed to hold the greatest promise. I felt that somewhere on Antler Mountain near Grouse Creek there must be a downward extension of the old, rich Heron Channel. If my theory was correct, gold should be found on some of the small creeks and gulches which flow along Antler Mountain into Grouse or Antler Creeks.

Yet two years went by before I set out for Barkerville in the late fall of 1932; and it was not until the summer of 1935 that I found myself testing a small creek flowing from Antler Mountain into Antler Creek. It was obviously unworked and unexplored; and my first test gave me nearly a half ounce of coarse nugget gold. After staking a lease I put in a sluice box and then, working only a few hours shovelling in gravels from the bedrock which was near the surface at this point, I took out nearly two ounces of the same gold. This was later attested to by Joe Wendle as being undeniably Grouse Creek gold. He was most impressed and excited about this find.

Later Ken Carpenter and I went into partnership and prospected there for the remainder of that season, and off and on for several more seasons. I have often thought that had I not found gold that very first day, right where my theories led me to suspect it should be, my life might have been an entirely different story. For many years after this I prospected in and around Grouse Creek, but sad to relate, the Heron Channel remains today as deeply hidden as ever.

That late fall of 1932 I decided to stay in Barkerville for at least part of the winter and rented a cabin from Dan McLellan. "Uncle Dan's" cabin was on the far, upper end of the street and, I later learned, was one of the oldest buildings of the town. The townspeople joke with all newcomers by saying that if you live in Barkerville for two weeks you are committed to it for life. This has been proved many times to be true. I, too, had not been there long before falling under the spell of Barkerville, its people and history, and of the glorious surrounding countryside.

There were perhaps two or three hundred people living in Barkerville that winter of 1932–33. The town had several stores; the Barkerville Meat Market, Lee Chong's grocery, Campbell's store—which was in the original Hudson's Bay Post—Nichol's Hotel, the Kelly Hotel, McKinnon's store, the post office, the telegraph office, the present St. Saviour's Church, and another church which was actually one of the buildings moved down from Richfield. Mrs. Wendle looked after this church for many years. Besides these there were the Chinese Masonic Hall, the Masonic Hall, at least four cafes, the jail and the Theatre Royal.

One of the curious things about most mining towns is the large number of dogs that roam the streets seemingly untended and unowned. This was true of Barkerville. Packs of them would meet the returning prospectors and trappers on the outskirts and follow them to their cabins, barking, jumping and yipping at their heels. They kept us awake half the night with their noise, until many a man developed a lifelong indifference to dogs if not indeed an outright dislike. I recall one night when they had been particularly noisy, barking back and forth to one another. Suddenly there came the rarely heard, long eerie howl of a timber wolf, followed by another. As if by magic the dogs of the town were silenced.

During the winter months there were numerous activities in the town. There were bridge clubs, teas, church services and bazaars, parties, dances, sledding and skiing. The skiing parties were a particular attraction. A group of us, young men and women, gathered many times on bright, moonlit nights to go on a ski tour. Most often we started at the farther end of the old street, skiing up the long, narrow valley past the Richfield Courthouse and Summit Rock to Groundhog Basin. Here we stopped and lighted a bonfire where we made coffee and drank it with the lunches we had brought. Sometimes we had a wiener roast and stayed for a time skiing up and down the slopes of Groundhog Basin. Then we would be off again, heading for the mountain slopes of Proserpine, from where we would reach Antler Road, skimming down its two-mile slope past Cochran's house, and so home again. The round trip was a distance of eight to twelve miles. They were nights to remember.

On skis we climbed the hills and traversed the flat stretches, running the long mountain slopes over the crisp snow, now in shadow, now lighted by a bright winter moon. This was the first time that I had heard the term "ski heil" called out, as we started down the slopes from Summit Rock or Conklin Hill. On these tours I can remember, among others, Harry Bradley, Max Grady, my brother Ben, Lil Magee, a young Swedish chap, Nels Anderson, and Lorna Boyd. Lorna's uncles were the sons of the original owners of Cottonwood House, built in the early 1860s. In 1934 a ski hill was constructed in Barkerville, at the far end of the town on the slopes to the left at the old Black Jack Mine, and that winter there was a ski meet with participants from Quesnel, Prince George and even Vancouver. Lil Magee won the ladies' ski championship and many trophies. Tom Mobraaten won the men's championship. He was later ski pro at Hollyburn Ridge, Vancouver.

The dances were held in the old Theatre Royal. In those days it had the stage and original heavy velvet curtains and dressing rooms with large ornamental mirrors and many other items belonging to the days when it had been built in 1869. Later this building was torn down to make room for the present community hall. At that time these priceless items were auctioned off to raise funds for the new hall. The townspeople spoke of this with deep regret, even years later. During the process of tearing it down it was revealed that five different floors had been laid successively on top of the original one.[1] The theatre was used as a community hall, and no charge was levied to hold a dance or party there. Anyone could at any time use it for whatever purpose he chose. The dances were a popular part of the life of Barkerville. At that time Mary McArthur was considered to be the Belle of Barkerville and at the dances the Belle of the Ball. She was pretty and vivacious, an excellent dancer and, like her brother Gordon, possessed a marvellous sense of humour. Her cousins, Mildred and Marge Tregillus, were also most popular at the dances. They were pretty young women, with an exceptionally good sense of rhythm that made them wonderful dancers.

Before the Theatre Royal was torn down, a farewell dance was held in the old building. Here we were all gathered, when on the stroke of midnight, what should happen but the old bell broke from its moorings, and came clattering down to land on the floor at the feet of the dancers, narrowly missing Howard Harris's head!

Early in the thirties my brother Ben came to Barkerville. He prospected, too, but his main interest lay in trapping and hunting. By 1934 we had built and comfortably furnished a cabin of our own, supplying it with a woodshed and overhanging roof and porch. This was on the Antler Road, a bit above Cochran's house. Nestled in among the trees, and with a lovely view, it was quiet, removed from the town and yet near enough for convenience.

Those were happy years in the cabin and in Barkerville, and we became more deeply aware of the countless attractions of the town and its wonderful people. We knew how much we enjoyed the variety of winter activities, and the marvel of the short summer months with the picnics, exploratory trips to favourite historic sites, and trips around the long chain of lakes some fourteen miles from Barkerville.

---

1. The sweepings from these floors when panned down yielded a considerable amount of gold dust!

A favourite picnic spot on the top of Mount Murray was reached by following the Bowron Lake Road for about three miles, then taking a trail through the trees on the right, and by gradual ascent through the Jack pine and the alpine meadows up to the summit. From here one could look along the main streets of Barkerville, and by looking back could see Bowron Lake and River, and the top end of Isaac and Indian Point Lakes, which were part of the Bowron Lake chain. On any Sunday morning a half dozen or more of us would pack a lunch and take off on this inspiring trip; or we might go to Summit Rock, past the Richfield Courthouse and past the old workings of the sixties, to the huge rock which served as a landmark on the road from Stanley to Richfield and Barkerville up to 1885.

I made these trips often with Charlie Ross who was as keenly interested as I in the old trails and the early days. His father had been one of the pioneers of the Chilcotin. On one of the tramps past Summit Rock, Charlie and I came across a stretch of road about three-quarters of a mile long which had been built in 1864, but never used. When constructing the road, the men had somehow miscalculated, reaching a point where the grade would have been too steep for the pony expresses and stage and freight teams. So this section of the road was abandoned and another piece built at a lower grade. We could see the outline of the original road clearly, and walked along its grass-covered length before returning to the trail we were on.

Another favourite place to visit in the summer months was the famous Lowhee Mine which at that time had been in operation for over seventy years and had progressed for a distance of nearly two miles through the mountains. The deep, wide trench sluiced out hydraulically over the years was an amazing and breathtaking sight.

Ben and I were fascinated by all these things, and we dreamed of building a lodge in Barkerville to provide accommodation for the visitors that Barkerville warranted. We pictured the skiing, hunting and fishing and the historic sites that would attract them. Besides this, I knew from personal observation that there was a wealth of historically valuable antiques in the homes of so many of the townspeople. There were countless Chinese articles, beautiful vases delicately painted and decorated, copper and brass vessels, Chinese reed flutes, old oriental Sam Suey bottles and ginger jars. Many of these had been brought in with the original owners from China in the sixties or even earlier into San Francisco or Victoria and thence to Barkerville. There were four-poster beds, manufactured in Barkerville and smoothed, polished and stained by hand; needlework, photographs, pictures and valuable old letters, stamps, ledgers and records. I felt that over the years some of these items might be acquired and preserved to fill a small museum of the Barkerville days. Ben and I did go so far as to cut and peel the logs with the intention of building a lodge but when we began to compute the probable cost we regretfully concluded that our dream must be postponed. The lodge, in fact, never materialized, but through the years it remained in the back of my mind as something I would some day attempt. I began to read every available scrap of material on the history of Barkerville and talked and listened even more than formerly to the old-timers who had come into the camp in the nineties, eighties and even the seventies—such men as Bill Brown, Dune McIntyre, Jimmy Delhanty, Andy Campbell, Bert Parsons, John Houser, Fred Tregillus, Joe Wendle and the descendants of the early miners. It is amazing to me now, in looking back, just how much accurate and authentic knowledge of the Cariboo and Barkerville, its history, people, life and accomplishments, I acquired in those first few years.

When, at the end of the prospecting season, I went hunting, it was not for game. My idea of recreation was to seek and find the many historic sites that were almost lost to sight and memory. There were, for example, the site of the old, long-since-destroyed town of Antler, the site of Grouse Town, and even some fragmentary ruins of Grouse Creek City; the small buildings on Antler Mountain which the Chinese had used while making shakes; old cabins and first cabins and ruins of old roadhouses. Charlie Ross, and also later Bill Ward, and I followed up all the old trails used by the first prospectors. Our first venture in this was finding and following the original trail from Barkerville to Antler where we found the old racetrack on Race Track Creek. Here were two unmarked graves surrounded by a small, white picket fence. We then went from Antler to Keithley. All these trips were rewarding and pleasurable experiences, and almost always we found some memento of earlier days.

One time in 1935 we were retracing the original trail past the town of Antler over the Snowshoe Plateau. We sat down to rest and placed our packs against a spruce tree, below the mouth of Nugget Gulch. As we rested we noticed an area under the spruce where no small woods plants grew. On tracing the area we observed it was in the shape of a headboard. We cleaned away the needles and twigs, and sure enough, there was a wooden headboard. It read:

IN LOVING MEMORY OF
HENRY J. LUCAS
DIED IN 1888

There was no evidence of a grave, so we rested the board against the tree and left it there. On returning to Barkerville some days later we learned the following: Henry Lucas had perished while crossing in winter over the Snowshoe Plateau between the towns of Antler and Keithley. His relatives in Chicago had sent the funds to have the board made and placed on the grave. His remains had been buried on the plateau. The man employed to pack the board to its assigned place had evidently taken it only to the spruce tree; and there it remained until found in 1935. In 1940 Joe Wendle paid to have the marker taken to the grave on the plateau, its original destination. It had taken fifty-two years for the headboard to be transported from Barkerville to the Big Snowshoe Plateau, a distance of approximately eighteen miles!

2
THE GOLD TRAILS

There's gold in the Cariboo! It was with these words, spoken by thousands and thousands of people in 1859, '60 and '61 that the story of Barkerville really begins. Men in California, Canada, and later England and even the Continent, were learning of gold in fabulous amounts in the Cariboo. The history of British Columbia from 1858 on is studded with the names of thousands of men who found gold, until anyone reading it would think this great territory was one immense gold field!

As early as 1858 Kinahan Cornwallis published a book entitled *The New Eldorado, or British Columbia.* The amazing thing about this book is a map it contains on which is printed *Supposed Gold Regions.* These three words appeared in nearly every part of the Cariboo where gold was actually discovered two years later. This illustrated the belief of the prospectors that the trail of fine gold in the Fraser and Thompson would eventually lead to heavy deposits of coarse gold in the mountains at the headwaters of these rivers.

At that time British Columbia and Vancouver Island were remote colonies of Great Britain. Most of the vast interior of British Columbia was as yet unexploited by White settlers. Yet in the short space of ten years, from 1858 to 1868, literally thousands of men trekked through this great interior wilderness, creating settlements and towns, ranches and farms. The event that brought these fantastic numbers of men into this hinterland was the epic Cariboo Gold Rush. The greatest part of this colourful event centred on Williams Creek. It was here on the Creek, fifty-eight miles from the present town of Quesnel, that Barkerville came into being. During the 1800s it was the flourishing centre of the Cariboo's mining activities, and with variations in its fortunes, it continued to hold its place as a stable community until 1958.

These thousands of gold seekers, rather than the early fur traders and Hudson's Bay men, were instrumental, too, in the opening up

The lure of the Cariboo—gold! Barkerville Museum P6567

of roads throughout this vast area, most of which was accessible only by water and by following the Indian trails on foot, horse or mule. The need for roads to the goldfields, and the subsequent building of them, also did much to prevent the political disruption of the western part of British North America. The fact that Governor Douglas saw this need and instigated the building of the Cariboo Road, thus establishing it as the main line to the goldfields, was a great factor in firmly establishing British law and justice north of the forty-ninth parallel. By this time hundreds of men were arriving daily from the United States, and they came not only by steamboat from San Francisco to Victoria and thence to Yale, but also hundreds more came via Fort Colville in the United States through the Okanagan Valley to Kamloops and so north to the Cariboo.

But all were seeking the same thing—gold!

Although in 1858 gold was still being mined at Hope and Yale, the rush that started on the Lower Fraser had already taken men to the Thompson and Similkameen Rivers, and to countless streams, bars and benches everywhere in the lower part of the province. Miners were making as much as twenty dollars a day on the Similkameen and getting coarser gold than elsewhere. They were mining for gold at Lillooet—then called Cayoosh—on the Fraser River (the ancestral and unceded territories of the St'át'imcets people). But what is significant is that in 1858 three hundred ounces of gold was taken from Cedar Point, the mouth of a stream that flows into Quesnel Lake. Cedar Point was the boat landing of the fur brigade taking furs from the Quesnel and Cariboo Lake areas into Fort Alexandria, more than a hundred miles north of Lillooet.

By 1859 almost a thousand men were mining for gold between Fort Alexandria, Fort George and Quesnel Forks. In 1860 large quantities of gold were found in the Horsefly River which, too, flows into Quesnel Lake. Then, in the summer of 1860, gold was discovered on the shores of Cariboo Lake. Here men, travelling to and from their destinations over its great expanse on rafts, were making as much as two hundred dollars a day. All this before any fabulous strikes had been made!

3
THE GREAT PLATEAU

George Weaver and W.R. (Doc) Keithley were two of the men who, by 1860, had arrived as far north as the Cariboo River. That summer they travelled up the river in a northeasterly direction for a distance of about twenty miles. Here they found a convenient crossing and continued in the same direction for another three or four miles, taking test pans as they went. They came upon a gold-bearing creek which flowed into Cariboo Lake from the north. This creek, named after Keithley, was not a rich source of gold compared with others. However, dozens of parties followed and staked claims there and in the surrounding area, and it became one of the famous creeks of the Cariboo. The settlement of Keithley sprang up almost overnight and continued for many years as a prominent supply centre. It wasn't until a year after Keithley's discovery that the original creek bed was found on bench land some distance from its present flow. It was then that mining in the gold-bearing gravels truly began.

George Weaver and Doc did a considerable amount of work in opening up the creek, in the hope that it might prove rich enough to warrant putting in a plant. However, this was not to be at that time and they, along with two other men, John Rose and an American, Ben MacDonald, decided to explore further.

The men wanted to have enough supplies to last them at least a month, to provide for ample time to go on a fairly extended prospecting and scouting trip up Keithley Creek and farther if necessary. They must have flour for bannock, some dried fruit, beans, rice, tea, salt and sugar. Most prospectors depended on wild game to furnish them with fresh meat. The food supply alone was weighty. Besides this they would need tarps for shelter, bedrolls and, at the very least, an axe, pick, shovel, gold pan and firearms.

At last, in the late fall of 1860, each one weighted down by sixty to seventy pounds of supplies, they set out from Keithley. Fortunately, at this time of year the mosquitoes and blackflies were gone, also much of the underbrush was stripped of constricting leaves and vines. But even so there were obstacles to contend with. It was an up-hill climb through a narrow ravine, blocked by windfalls, over which they must clamber or find a way around. At times the windfalls were lying every which way, making it almost impossible to traverse. They came at last to a branch of Keithley Creek, later named Snowshoe Creek. Continuing in the same manner and direction, they followed the creek to its source, a distance of six or seven miles. From here they could see above them a crest of land which proved to be a great, extended plateau. Taking off their heavy packs they stood for some minutes in silent awe, gazing at the breathtaking scene before them: the country to the west and northwest was of a fairly level nature, but to the north and east were great, rugged mountains, and far below, rolling hills, valleys and ravines. From this magnificent height of land, the creeks flowing through the ravines and valleys looked unreal, so small and far away they seemed. The men could see that the plateau divided the watershed of the Cariboo River and Lake from that of those creeks and valleys which they now beheld for the first time. This to them was most significant. Any one of the creeks could be gold-bearing and could lead to an entirely new source of gold. One can imagine with what eagerness they began crossing the plateau, and how each might suggest this or that likely-looking stream un-til, having come to a decision, they began descending to the new un-touched valleys far below.

It was much harder to get down with their heavy, unwieldy packs than it had been to climb. The packs pressed against them and forced their pace in descending. Here were more windfalls, but there were also sheer drops, where creeks had cut off great slices of land, leaving tangled brush and a rubble of clay and rocks. At last the feat was accomplished and they reached a creek which flowed through a narrow, rock canyon. This was to become known as Antler Creek, renowned in the Cariboo for its gold and its history.

They began to examine it, and at once found gold on either side of the creek on a limestone dike, some so close to the surface that no digging was needed. One of them took a pan worth $75! Another $100! It was gold such as never before had been seen in the Colony.

Some was actually in plain view in exposed pockets on the wa-ter-worn bedrock. It was rusty in colour due to oxidization of the iron concentrates, and for this reason was referred to as "sunburn gold."

The party's excitement was such that none felt they could even dare take the time to prepare camp for the night. But darkness began falling all too soon, and the sky was dull and overcast, making it necessary to prepare a proper shelter. One of the men built a fire, then behind the fire two posts were driven into the ground and the intervening space filled with logs, thus forming a solid back, permitting heat from the fire to reflect into the campsite. Another rigged up a frame from trees and covered it with branches to provide a fairly adequate roof. Additional fuel was brought in and water carried from the creek. Then each put his bedroll in place and began taking out supplies for a meal—the first meal in this land which was to become known to thousands as the fabulous goldfields of the Cariboo.

Each of these men had already been on long, arduous trails from Yale or Kamloops to Alexandria. How far each had come, how long each had searched for the nuggets that now lay before their eyes in the gold pan! Before darkness deepened, they re-examined their gold and made eager plans for the next day's work. Then all slept on this night which was in essence the beginning of the town of Antler, and the beginning, too, of Grouse Town, Richfield, Barkerville, Van Winkle and Stanley.

It was a shock the next morning to discover a foot of snow on the ground. But long before noon most of it would be gone. Besides, so much had yet to be done. There was more prospecting to be accomplished before they would know for sure where to stake their claims. They were determined that no one should know of this great find until they had properly established their claims on it.

The days now were quite short, and as soon as it was light, they were off to dig and pan, explore, test and stake. They continued in much the same way, using their first shelter. These were quiet days, filled with work and purpose, and with weariness at night. Rose and MacDonald gave serious consideration to the necessity of building a cabin before the heavy winter snows really began. Later they did in fact build one. It was small, as were most first cabins in those early days, only eight by ten feet in size. They built it of spruce and balsam logs, with a clay and rock fireplace at one end and with a split-log door at the other. Not elaborate, it nonetheless provided wonderfully adequate shelter against the severe winter days that followed.

It was not long before the men had to return to Keithley for winter supplies. But they realized that there was an easier route back that would avoid going up to the plateau and then down again. About a half-mile from Discovery Rock, the spot on Antler Creek where they had first found gold, there was a long flat which would take them due south, practically straight in the direction of Keithley. They travelled along this flat for about three miles, which brought them close to the Swift River and thence to MacMartin Creek. MacMartin, its discoverer, was working on the creek and they followed his trail to Keithley. In this way the trip from Keithley back to Antler followed the natural grade of Keithley Creek, then down MacMartin and up the Swift River. It cut down considerably on the steep climbs and reduced the miles to fourteen in all between the two centres. This was the route that would be used in the years following.

Had they but known it, the day that Rose and MacDonald, Keithley and George Weaver left Antler for winter supplies was the last of their quiet days of work on the creek. At Keithley the word of their strike somehow leaked out. Despite their efforts to keep their secret, the news spread, and by midwinter dozens of parties set out from Keithley, trekking over five and six feet of snow to Antler to stake claims. Many of them went by way of the plateau, thus giving it the name of Snowshoe Plateau. So much excitement was stirred up that claims were staked over claims, giving rise to much dispute. Men lived in holes dug in the snow. By the spring of 1861, the creek was solidly staked. Houses, cabins, even stores and other businesses mushroomed near the mining area. Later these were ordered to be removed as the ground belonged to the men who had staked there. Eventually they were completely destroyed by mining operations.

By May 1861, there were twelve hundred men mining between Quesnel Forks and Keithley and at Antler. Small companies of two or three men were formed to meet the expenses of mining. Even though there was four feet of snow on the banks of Antler Creek, reports of the wealth of the creek were already in circulation. One company had a gold output of $900 for two days' work, another $300 a day per man.

Later on in the season George Weaver and Doc Keithley put in a four-mile-long ditch to carry water to their ground. It was reported to have cost from $15,000 to $20,000, and their gold output more than paid for the expense. Ben MacDonald, after clearing a small fortune, sold his claim to his partner for $4,000 and left for California. The names of only a few of the men and companies that did exceptionally well on Antler this first year were: Coote & Company, Smith, Cain,

MacLean, Hazelton, Rutherford, Sweeny, Whitney, Moreland, Montgomery, Millar and Rose, Bergert & Company and Hendrick. The Bergert & Company's claim was reputed to be the richest on the creek, averaging $200 to $400 a day. In one little crevice in the bedrock, this company took out sixty to seventy ounces of gold. Many men made as much as $100 a day, and no one made less than $40 a day.

As early as May 1861, a small sawmill was established at Antler near the flat where the men had started back for Keithley the previous fall. From then on this stretch of ground was called Sawmill Flat. All the equipment for the sawmill was brought by pack animal over the narrow trails from New Westminster. There was a constant demand for lumber, and the man who owned the mill, R.P. Baylor, did a thriving business for some years. Another man, I.B. Nason, later became associated with this sawmill. He was a well-to-do young man who had come, like hundreds of others, in search of gold. He was to have an important place in the Cariboo for many years to come.

J.C. Beedy was one of the first to put up a store at Antler in the spring of 1861. He also was keenly interested in the mining and was to do a great deal of exploration work throughout the Cariboo in the next twenty years.

By July 1861, Antler town already boasted over sixty houses and businesses. Very shortly it was possible to procure even luxury items in the stores, such things as could be obtained nowhere else inland beyond New Westminster. One example of this was champagne, which sold at $12 a bottle. In a country rich in gold strikes, doubtless champagne suited many occasions to celebrate good luck.

The *Victoria Colonist* sent up a correspondent who wrote under the name "Argus" to cover the news at Antler. In one of his "Letters from Antler," written August 17, 1861, were these comments:

> Robberies are not infrequent in Antler. Recently $130 in gold dust and two pistols were taken from Cameron's Golden Age Saloon. A slight stabbing affair is also noted. Watson and Taylor's Minstrels are still performing at Antler.

The gold in Antler Creek extended downstream through its narrow valley for a mile and a half; and mining by ground sluice and rocker was carried on extensively for many years.

4
THE RICH FIELDS

Of the hundreds of men who travelled over the snow trails to Antler Creek in the midwinter and very early spring of 1861 to stake claims, a goodly proportion found on their arrival that all the rich ground was already claimed. These men began immediately to look elsewhere. Some of them travelled on down Antler to Lower Antler Creek, others went up the creek and investigated various streams flowing into it. Still others left the creek entirely and discovered new streams and new sources of gold. As a result of all this, during the early spring and summer of 1861 dozens of different rich gold-bearing creeks were discovered almost simultaneously. Many creeks and streams flowing into them were opened up, explored, tested, worked or abandoned, and were given names by which they are still known. A few of the dozens of such creeks are Cunningham, Nugget Gulch, Wolfe, China, Beggs Gulch, Guyet, Downey, Quartz, Canadian and White Grouse. But there were, besides these, four creeks which were to become not only the nucleus but the chief source of gold in the rush that followed the discovery of Antler. These were Williams, Lightning, Lowhee and Grouse Creeks.

The first of these, Williams Creek, was discovered in February 1861. On different dates during that month several separate parties of men, learning that Antler Creek was solidly staked, decided to push on past Discovery Rock, where gold had first been found, and continue up the creek. After coming across a small stream, which was later to be called Racetrack Creek, they turned right and climbed the mountain slope, to find themselves on a broad plateau. Because it was devoid of all timber, they named it Bald Mountain Plateau. Among the first in these separate parties were William Dietz and two companions, Edward Stout and his partner, and Vital La Force and Michael Burns.

By the time Edward Stout and his partner arrived at the western end of the plateau it was growing dark, but they could still make out a creek winding through a narrow valley about a mile below them.

They decided to camp for the night in the snow and investigate the stream next day. That evening as they sat before their fire, drinking tea and discussing the possibilities of discovering gold, they suddenly could make out the glimmer of a campfire through the trees in the valley far below them.

The campfire was that of William Dietz and his two companions, who had arrived at the creek late the night before and had spent the day prospecting. Up until the time that they had made their camp and lit a fire to cook a meal, the Dietz party had found nothing but ten to thirty-cent pans. After they had eaten, "Dutch Bill" Dietz decided to have one more try, and he travelled up the creek until he found a bare bedrock outcropping. A panful of gravel was washed without finding colours. Dietz then tried a pan from the side near a high ledge. This yielded him a dollar to the pan. He continued taking pans of frozen gravel and by thawing them in the stream managed to pan them down, and his good luck persisted. However, his companions, perhaps because of their long day of failure, did not seem to credit his find and were determined to return to Quesnel Forks. The next day Bill Dietz staked a claim, even though he had wished to take more time to prospect and assure himself of having the best on this new creek. He little knew that history was being made at that moment nor that his name would be given to what was shortly to become the world-renowned Williams Creek.

Edward Stout and his partner, and shortly afterwards Michael Burns and Vital La Force, being the next of the parties to arrive, prospected up and down the creek, though the whole valley was covered with seven and eight feet of snow. These men also staked claims before being compelled to snowshoe back to Keithley for supplies.

By the time the handful of first discoverers had returned to the creek with sufficient supplies and tools to begin working their claims, they found that dozens of men had already staked claims that extended on both sides of the creek to a narrow rock canyon about a mile downstream. Prospectors coming into Antler had learned of this new find and immediately set out for Dutch Bill's or William's Creek, as they named it.

At that time the nearest mining recording office was about seventy miles away at Williams Lake, southwest of Quesnel Forks. Gold Commissioner Philip Nind was flooded with work as men snowshoed over the mountains in droves to record claims. In this rush of arrivals an American named Thomas Brown had the distinction of being the first to record a claim on Williams Creek.

In the next month or so—through March, April and well into May—the men on Williams Creek were hard pressed to get the essential work done preparatory to mining. They had to clear their claims of heavy timber, build rockers or sluice boxes from the raw trees to the finished product, and set up shelters for themselves. The tools they possessed were of the minimum; and logs had to be split and planed to supply any lumber needed. It was hard, grinding work and, as the snow melted, more work was created by the rush of water in the creek. Piles of logs jammed up, damming the water until removed, and tree stumps measuring two and three feet in diameter had to be cut up and pulled out. At last, towards the middle of May, the men began mining in earnest. Some ground-sluiced, others sank holes or shafts, and still others drove open cuts straight into the bank of the creek.

As spring suddenly changed into summer, the excitement on the creek grew as one and then another began taking out gold. Of course, with the summer came blackflies, mosquitoes, tangled underbrush and flooding waters. At first the actual evidence of gold in their pans did much to alleviate the torments of early summer. But for all that, during those very first few weeks after finding the gold, a kind of discouragement settled over the creek. Many of the miners were not finding gold in the quantities of which they had dreamed or that they expected. A few were getting better than wages, but the majority were not. The creek for some time was called by the disgruntled miners, "Humbug Creek." This is probably the only time in the history of Williams Creek that the word discouragement could properly be used, and even then, the condition was of short duration.

The gold the miners were finding was on a hard, blue clay about eight to ten feet below the surface. One day on the Abbott and Jourdan claim, Abbott was working alone while his partner was away getting provisions. The thought came to him that he would try to pierce below this blue clay, which up to then had been considered to be, in effect, the bedrock. Upon doing so he found gravels so rich that by the time Jourdan returned forty-eight hours later, Abbott was able to produce fifty ounces of smooth, waterworn nuggets!

It was in that significant hour when Abbott first penetrated below the blue clay that the fabulous success of Williams Creek truly began.

From then on all the miners on the creek dug below this blue clay to get their gold and the richness of their findings reads like a fairy tale. The amount of gold taken out of Williams Creek in the weeks following Abbott's discovery was on a scale of riches unrealized and hitherto undreamed of on other creeks. Two or three hundred ounces a day was not at all uncommon. Steele and Company had actually taken out four hundred and nine ounces of gold in one day! As early as August 1861, Abbott's Company was reported to have made an operating profit of $80,000. Both the Abbott and Steele companies for a time reckoned their gold in pounds—twenty-five and thirty pounds of gold in a day! The Dawson Company had, from the gravels below the clay, taken out fifty-six ounces of gold, then on reaching the bedrock below these gravels, took out a further three hundred ounces!

Meanwhile the original discoverers' claims, though not as rich as these at first, soon were producing anywhere from fifty to one hundred and fifty ounces daily. For some reason William Dietz, although he had discovered the creek, was not as successful as the others, particularly in that first year. By November he had returned to Victoria, not a wealthy man, sick of a malady he had picked up in the Cariboo, and very much discouraged. Yet in the government records the Dietz claim is shown, in an overall total output over the years, to have surpassed that of Abbott and Jourdan.

The great amounts of gold that the miners were recovering presented them, oddly enough, with a new problem. Their first concern was for the safety of their treasure. No banks existed, and there were few places where it was safe enough to leave it. Some of the miners buried it in tin cans in the floors of their cabins or tents or under the roots of large trees or stumps. When the amount of gold became large it was packed to the workings each morning and back to the camp in the evening and slept with until it could be disposed of to gold buyers.

Williams Creek now was alive with men seeking gold. Hundreds of them trekked over from Antler, and the whole creek from the canyon up and on both banks was solidly packed with miners and mining claims. Those unable to find suitable ground spent the entire season prospecting. Many, though unable to find anything to mine, were in the end able to secure a good prospect for the next season. Some who were fortunate enough to have money even managed to buy an interest in a paying mine. No man wanted to hire out for wages alone, and often if a company needed extra men the only way open to it was to give a man an interest. During the month of August, Abbott and Jourdan sold an interest in their mine for $8,000. Later other companies did the same. This practice also had the added advantage of allowing the company to secure an extra claim on ground that it knew to be rich, as only one claim was allowed to each man.

During the month of August, the rain drove down almost constantly. Often a twenty-four, even a forty-eight-hour downpour filled the creeks with mud slides containing huge boulders, trees and stumps. A particularly heavy freshet took out all the flumes on Keithley Creek and some on Antler. The rains, coupled with the heavy traffic of men and supplies leaving Keithley for Antler and Williams Creeks, made the trails between the first two towns practically impassable. Nonetheless the pack animals, laden with provisions and equipment, did make their way to the mining fields. As many as twenty pack trains passed through Quesnel Forks in the last week of August. The first one to reach Williams Creek was that of A.G. Norris, who arrived before the middle of August. His arrival marked the beginning of the town of Richfield, which this portion of Williams Creek was now fittingly named. With Norris's arrival, and the growing need of services, merchants already in the Cariboo, as well as some men who were not doing so well at the mining, began making plans to build and open stores and hotels.

The weather brightened slightly for a few days in September, but soon it turned wet and cold again. By the middle of the month the miners awakened on many mornings to find an inch of snow on the ground. This usually melted quickly, but the ice on the water in the mornings, and a chill nip in the air, even when the sun shone, bespoke a winter to be reckoned with all too soon. By this time there were nearly four hundred men on the creek. Those who were mining expected to be able to continue work till mid-October, as had the men at Antler the year before. Nevertheless, by the end of September many miners and almost all those who still were prospecting, had either left or were making preparations to go.

About eighty men remained at Richfield that first winter of 1861. They continued mining through the cold, wet, icy days as long as the creek remained open. But soon bitter winter descended, covering the hills and ravines with snow and their workings with ice.

The miners began chinking their cabins, cutting firewood, and otherwise preparing to winter it out on the creek. Some of those who had sunk shafts even planned to continue mining through the winter. There were last-minute trips to Antler for provisions, clothing and ammunition. Once at Antler they often remained for some days, talking to friends there and in some measure satisfying their hunger for reports of the luck of other miners and news of the outside world. Antler offered a warm, cozy atmosphere and a sense of well-being for the wintering miners as they sat in a proper eating place or stood at a bar once more forgetting for a while the snow and cold.

Meanwhile those miners who had left were arriving daily in Yale, New Westminster, Victoria and San Francisco. With them they carried an air of romance and adventure. Friends and relatives listened for hours, spellbound, to their tales of the Cariboo. Some of the things they heard were scarcely credible, yet the miners had only to display the gold they brought with them and all doubt disappeared.

When the men from the Abbott and Jourdan Company reached Victoria on October 25th, they had with them $80,000 worth of gold. Each man carried his portion of gold in a canvas bag slung over his back. They were met at the Hudson's Bay wharf by agents of the Wells Fargo Company, who were to take it under their care. As the men left the wharf they were followed by a crowd of awestruck people. Fascinated by what they had heard, the townsmen couldn't take their eyes off the bags of gold. Even after they had seen the shipment placed securely in a safe many remained, seeming unable to do anything but gaze in silence at the safe that held the gold. In the hearts of most there arose a firm resolve to go to the mines come the next year.

In the *Victoria Colonist,* one of the newspapers which had from its beginning kept abreast of news of the Cariboo Gold Rush, many items appeared. How romantically they read! In the October 7th issue, under the heading ARRIVAL OF THE OTTER (the steamship that brought Cariboo passengers and others from New Westminster to Victoria), were these comments:

> There were forty-five passengers and $100,000 in gold dust. On September 17th Steele and Company, whose claims adjoin those of the Dawson and Abbott Companies, cleaned up four hundred and seventy-five ounces, or $7,600, in gold dust in one day! This statement

comes authenticated by a respectable citizen who saw the clean-up in question, and we can vouch for its truth.

In the October 14th issue:

There were one hundred and thirty passengers and $150,000 in gold dust. Fifty of the passengers were from the Cariboo. The amount of gold dust by this arrival is the greatest ever received by any one conveyance from British Columbia. Three Italians brought $12,000 in gold which they had obtained from three weeks' mining. Two miners had $20,000 each, mostly in nuggets from a half to seven ounces in size. They retain their interest in the claim.

On the day that Abbott had arrived, the *Colonist* announced that there were seventy-two passengers from the Cariboo and $250,000 in gold dust!

At the end of the mining season of 1861 the recorded output of gold was over $2,600,000, and almost all of this came from the Cariboo.

5
SUCCESS AND DESPAIR

By the first week in March 1862, many miners began returning to Richfield on Williams Creek, and these were shortly followed by scores of prospectors in search of gold. The whole creek had a lively atmosphere as men began to erect houses and business establishments. Many of those who had remained had already sunk some prospecting shafts on the hillsides, and now others followed their example. Although by the middle of March there was still over four feet of snow, the weather was so mild that the ice had gone from the creek, and it was possible for all the claims to be worked.

Reports were already reaching Richfield that hundreds of men at Yale, Lytton, Victoria, and even as far away as San Francisco, were making preparations to leave for the Cariboo gold diggings. By April these men had started out. Hundreds of them had no pack animals after they left transportation at Yale. They travelled by foot with their provisions and what tools they could manage slung in packs on their backs. This was soon to create a sorry state of affairs as provisions were in such short supply that prices soared, and in fact for some weeks it was impossible to get supplies anywhere at any price.

Besides these hundreds of men on the way up, nearly five hundred men had wintered in the Cariboo on the various creeks and in the towns. To do any business regarding their claims or to examine any mining records the men all had to travel to Gold Commissioner Nind at Williams Lake. This created a great hardship for them and an overwhelming amount of work for Nind. All were of the opinion that no man could carry out the amount of work expected of him, and that he should have the help of at least four deputy gold commissioners and four magistrates. Early in May a leave of absence that Nind had asked for was granted, and Thomas Elwyn was appointed in his place. Elwyn suggested that the Cariboo be divided into two districts, with a gold commissioner serving each. His advice was heeded, and as a result he was appointed to the eastern section, where most of

A Pack Train at the Cottonwood House. Barkerville Archives Acc. 1991.412 Boyd Collection

the mining was carried on, and which consequently had the heaviest load of work, and Peter O'Reilly was assigned the western section. As a temporary measure Elwyn rented a building at Quesnel Forks and carried on the government business for four or five weeks from this site. It was apparent, however, that the office should be situated at Richfield; and it was here that he subsequently came, and thus became the first gold commissioner on Williams Creek.

By the end of May more than twenty business establishments were completed at Richfield, and their owners were awaiting supplies to stock their stores, restaurants and saloons. For a short time two or three restaurants had been able to sell meals and liquor. But by now, there were five hundred prospectors and miners on the creek. The shortage of supplies that had begun to be felt in April as far south as Lillooet was causing grave concern. At one time the only supplies to be had at Williams Creek were in the hands of Steele & Company, and most of the miners were forced to go to Antler. Here, as elsewhere, the prices were outrageous. Flour sold readily at $1 to $1.25 a pound, salt $1.50 for five pounds, bacon $1.50 to $1.75 a pound, sugar $1.50 a pound and tea and coffee $3 and $2.50 a tin, respectively. Rubber boots had been quoted at $50 a pair but none were in stock. Even such necessities as candles were $3 a dozen and matches $5 a dozen boxes. This worked a double hardship, as men who had arrived with a small amount of provisions on their backs and a little money put aside for prospecting in no time at all ran out of both. The only way some of these survived was by a helping hand from someone better supplied than themselves or by taking any wild meat they were able to get. Many left the Cariboo then, never to return.

The new gold commissioner, Thomas Elwyn, rescinded Nind's earlier layover of the claims to June 1st, and now extended the time to July 1st. As he observed the shortages and the hardships accompanying them, he felt it was not fair to ask men to rush back into such conditions. According to the *Mining Act*, a miner must live on his claim continuously in order to hold it. A winter layover was a general leave of absence for six months granted by the gold commissioner. With Elwyn's extension, the claims were now safe for another month. However, the hundreds of men on the creek who had observed the vacated claims and felt sure many would not return to retrieve them were bitterly disappointed by this new order. It meant a wait of another month and prospecting in and around the area of the claims with little money or supplies.

But the trails were lined with pack trains on their way to the mines; there were several cattle drives making their way from Oregon through Fort Colville and Kamloops and on up the perilous route to bring fresh meat to the miners. By mid-June the situation eased considerably as these at last reached their destination.

During the latter part of May and in the month of June the trails were in such a deplorable condition that many voiced complaints in the newspapers and elsewhere. One man wrote, "The government is forever talking of the road it is building to the mines, but in our opinion more attention and money should be spent on the trails up here." The route from Quesnel Forks to Keithley, Antler and Richfield was so heavily used that it was a constant marvel that it was able to accommodate the stream of miners, pack animals and cattle drives, while snow, ice, rain and frost added to the difficulty.

Meanwhile at Richfield reports of amazing clean-ups became more and more common as the season progressed. The names of William Cunningham, Steele, Abbott and Jourdan, Griffin, Michael Burns, and the Black Jack Claim (newly discovered) as well as the Tontine Company were only a few of those who had such fabulous success that news of their finds reached every ear. Once again reports of twenty-five hundred dollars for a half day's work from Steele

& Company, or over three hundred ounces in one day from the Black Jack or from other companies, new or old were, as in the season before, common.

A letter written by Thomas Elwyn to the Colonial Secretary at Victoria gives some idea of the immense activity going on in the Cariboo. Dated at Williams Creek on June 15th, 1862 it reads:

> At Antler five hundred men are preparing to mine but only a few companies are actually at work. There will be, I am satisfied, over one thousand men employed on the creek, and the yield of gold for this season will nearly equal the yield of the whole of the Cariboo last summer. Claims have been taken up both on the creek and on the banks for a distance of two miles which will pay $40 to $100 a day to the hand.
>
> I paid five shillings per pound for flour and six shillings per pound for bacon at the town of Antler (considered of very little importance last year.)...
>
> On my way from Antler to this place I passed within two and a half miles from the mouth of Grouse Creek, but my presence was so urgently required here that fearing a delay of some days I did not go up this creek.
>
> The yield of gold on Williams Creek is something almost incredible and the rich claims have risen to three times their market value of last winter. Only six companies are at present taking out gold but there are between five and six hundred men on the creek, sinking shafts and getting their claims into working order. Cunningham & Company have been working their claims for the past six weeks, and for the last thirty days have been taking out gold at the rate of three thousand dollars every twenty-four hours. In the tunnel owned by this company the average prospect is thirty-five ounces to the set. Messrs. Steele & Company have been engaged for the past ten days in making a flume but during the previous three weeks their claims yielded two hundred ounces a day. These figures are so startling that I should be afraid to put them on paper in a report for His Excellency's information were I not on the spot and know them to be the exact truth.

There is every possibility that before the end of this season there will be fifteen to twenty companies on this creek, the yield of whose claims will equal those above mentioned.

There are at present no provisions for sale here; but the prices hitherto have been about the same as at Antler Creek.

I expect to be detained here for five or six days settling mining disputes, after which I shall go to Lightning Creek...

A great many men, principally Canadians, are returning below. They are as a rule entirely ignorant of mining and came up here with a few pounds of provisions on their backs and hardly any money.

Considering the exorbitant prices...I hope that His Excellency will give his consent to Mr. Hankis and my constable receiving some extra allowance, or an increase in salary.

This letter was written in longhand and signed by Elwyn.

Sometime during the month of May a slight stir of excitement passed over Williams Creek when it was learned that Edward Stout had ventured below the narrow canyon and hit pay dirt on a gulch that flowed into the creek from the southwest. It was a wonderful find for Ned Stout who had had his share of misfortune on his trek up to the goldfields. He had been one of a group of twenty men who were confronted by some local Indigenous people while making their way through the Fraser Canyon. The siege by arrows and bullets lasted for two days, and by the time they were rescued by some other miners, all but five of the men had been killed, and these five men, including Stout, were very badly wounded.

Ned Stout had been considering the area below the canyon for some time. When he first dug into the gravels at the mouth of the new creek he came across the dark waterworn gold of Williams Creek; but on digging farther he discovered a different type of gold altogether. It was bright, jagged gold—a new, rich find.

Up until that date it was commonly believed that no gold could exist below the canyon but now, attracted by Stout's success, a fair number of miners decided to try their luck in this new area. The gold found on Williams Creek was on three different levels—to some extent on the surface, below the surface on the hard, blue clay and down through it to the gravels on bedrock where the pay was the richest. So these men took only a gold pan, pick and shovel at first, as they made their way through the heavy timber along the narrow banks of the canyon and on down about a half mile. Some of them went farther, to a comparatively flat stretch of the creek.

Among those men who first followed Ned Stout's example were two whose names were to become famous. These were William Barker and John A. Cameron.

Billy Barker of the Barker Claim. Image A-01144 courtesy Royal BC Museum and Archives

Born in England, Billy Barker had joined the Royal Navy when a young man. In 1861 he was aboard a British merchant ship when it stopped at Victoria. Here he learned even more of the gold rush than he had at the various ports of call. With every tale he heard, his excitement grew, with the result that he and a friend, "Sailor" Jack Edwards, deserted ship and set out for the goldfields.

John Cameron was born near Glengarry, Ontario. At the age of twenty-five he left his father's farm with his brother, Alan, and both became veterans of the California and of the Fraser River gold rushes. Both did well and returned home.

John Cameron was a man who, though of medium height and build, gave the appearance of strength and breadth. He had a high, broad forehead, brown wavy hair and blue eyes, and he wore almost a full beard. Seen in repose his face had a stern appearance, but when he was engaged in conversation, or at work at his mine, his

John A. Cameron. Image D-07951 courtesy Royal BC Museum and Archives

whole expression revealed his inner vitality. To his friends back home and to his relatives, he was a man who could beguile the hours away with stirring tales of the mining camps and the trails leading to them. It was at such times as these that his whole personality came into full play, revealing not a quiet, stern, hard-bitten miner, but a man eager and interested and alert to the people about him.

In the spring of 1862, he arrived at Williams Creek with his bride, the former Sophia Groves. She had come from the little town of Wales, not far from Cameron's place of birth.

John Cameron purchased a claim on Williams Creek and had located another but neither of these proved to be exceptionally rich. So when Ned Stout made his discovery both he and his partners were eager to follow it up and to find for themselves a claim below the canyon.

When Billy Barker followed the creek past the canyon and, farther down, came to a section of rimrock, he probably assumed that Williams Creek would have been turned aside from this, thus making for a concentration of gold. The shaft he put down was at a distance from the rimrock where one might suppose the deepest part of the buried channel to be. John Cameron, with his shaft more than half a mile farther down the creek, followed the same theory.

There was considerable speculation when these men and others began putting down their shafts. Many believed that their venture was doomed to failure, and there was a fair amount of good-natured ridicule and jesting. Nonetheless, their efforts were watched closely by all. Then on August 22nd, 1862, came the electrifying news that Barker had struck the pay at a depth of fifty-five feet. He was consistently sending up gold valued at five dollars a pan. This was good news enough, but when he reached bedrock at a depth of eighty feet and took out in one little crevice there the sum of one thousand dollars in gold in a matter of forty-eight hours the excitement knew no bounds. A few days later a group of miners in the Canadian Company struck pay. Then shortly afterwards John Cameron found evidence of his gold. With these discoveries all attention was now on the lower end of the creek below the canyon.

Early in July the new gold commissioner, Thomas Elwyn, arrived at Richfield. He began at once to make arrangements to have an office constructed. The log building when completed was sixteen by thirty feet in size and was partitioned to make an office and court room.

Mrs. John A. Cameron, née Margaret Sophia Groves. Image D-07952 courtesy Royal BC Museum and Archives

On the last day of August, Matthew Begbie, the circuit judge for the Cariboo, arrived and the first Grand Jury assembled at Richfield in the newly constructed courthouse.

By early September the miners below the canyon began building cabins there for themselves and for the men working with them. One of the first cabins to go up was that of John Cameron and his wife. She was gravely ill; and while all were jubilant at the new discoveries, these two could not help but think of the irony of a fate that had led them, after months of searching, to this rich gold mine, only to visit them with an illness that daily became more alarming. Nonetheless mining continued with unremitting success, and more and more shafts were sunk, and cabins sprang up in this new settlement, which soon became known as Cameron's Town, shortened eventually to Cameronton.

The Barker Company's shaft, and those shafts and cabins above and slightly below it, were fast becoming a nucleus of another small settlement. For quite a time it was variously referred to as Richfield, Lower Town, or Middletown, before the name of Barkerville was chosen.

It was evident to all who located claims below the canyon that, because of the extreme depth of overburden to bedrock, mining was going to be a much more expensive venture than formerly. Hundreds of feet of lumber were needed to lag the shafts. Pumps were needed to deal with water seepage and water wheels had to be built to run these pumps. Moreover, any miner considering putting down a shaft realized it must be anywhere from six weeks to two months before the rich pay would be reached. As a result of all this, there was a feeling of permanency in these new settlements from the outset. It was clear to all traders and merchants that, by their very nature, these could not become abandoned mining towns for many years.

During the month of September many of the overlander parties, who had just completed their long, heartbreaking trek across Canada, began arriving at Quesnel, then called Quesnelle Mouth. Most of the men of these parties decided to postpone their trip to the gold fields and to continue on their journey and reach the ocean while they still had funds enough to get there and to set themselves up for the winter. They were weary of travelling. A few, however, could not conceive of being so close and not at least visiting the mines. Two such men were A.L. Fortune and James Wattie. The latter's brother, William, had found employment building a log cabin and remained at Quesnel. The two men set out about the 15th of September. The trail was narrow, rough and muddy and they were able to make but fifteen miles a day. On the first day they stopped at a roadhouse at Cottonwood, leaving there an ox which had travelled the whole journey with them from the Red River Settlement. When they arrived at Williams Creek, they were pleased to learn that the richness of which they had heard and the quantities of gold taken out had not been exaggerated. They remained on the creek for eight days and visited with many of the miners.

The day they left, September 27th, there was a blinding snowstorm which followed them most of the way back and made the trip a hard one. However, both men felt that their efforts had been worthwhile, and that they had profited by gaining knowledge that would be of great use to them on their return the next spring. On their arrival at Quesnel they gave William Wattie a detailed account of what they had seen. The three men, there and then, made plans to seek their own fortunes on Williams Creek the next year.

The entire year of 1862 on Williams Creek was a paradox from beginning to end. Spring, and consequently the mining season, arrived three weeks earlier than usual. Yet hundreds of miners were unable to start work, partially due to the layover by Elwyn, and partially because of the serious shortage of provisions and equipment. Over a thousand men in all arrived on the creek, and yet surprisingly enough, relatively few new claims were worked. Many of the hundreds who came left in total discouragement, some even destitute. These same men met others who were just arriving. Thus there were prospectors journeying up the well-worn trails in eager expectation and at the same time weary and disillusioned men travelling down the same trails.

So despite the fact that this was the year that the deep diggings below the canyon were discovered, and such fabulous amounts of gold were taken from those shafts that had been completed to bedrock, 1862 was in many ways a sad year and one of discouragement to many miners.

Perhaps the saddest event of all was the death of Mrs. John Cameron. She had borne a baby daughter who had died at birth and had since contracted a fever. There were at the time four doctors on the creek, who had come seeking gold, but who treated the sick or injured. The doctor who was attending Mrs. Cameron did all in his power to save her, but his efforts failed.

John Cameron and his partner, Anderson, took Mrs. Cameron's body by sled over the frozen wastelands to Bella Coola and thence to Victoria, where he had a special coffin prepared, one which would preserve her body until it reached Ontario, where she was buried.

The total output of gold in 1862 was slightly more than the year before, but now there was definite knowledge of the certain richness of the creek and many more claims had been located and their owners were making plans for the next season's work.

Over a hundred miners in all elected to remain for the winter, some determined to mine in their shafts and tunnels as long as possible, if not throughout the entire winter. This winter miners had their own town of Richfield and need not travel the miles for provisions. Lieutenant Palmer, Deputy Commissioner of Lands and Works, had at the Grand Jury at Williams Creek in September officially named the settlement Richfield. For a time, there was some thought of giving it the name Elwyntown after the first gold commissioner, but Palmer thought that the name by which it had been called almost from the beginning was far more appropriate.

The miners banked and chinked up their cabins and with cheerful fires burning in their large stone fireplaces there was, despite isolation, a feeling of security and peace over the small settlement.

6
THE MINES AND THE MINERS

In the next year, 1863, there was such a vast difference in the whole atmosphere, attitude and even the physical appearance of Williams Creek that it was difficult to imagine it was the same place. Long before the middle of May over two thousand miners, prospectors, merchants, traders, express company representatives and packers arrived at Richfield, and most proceeded to the deeper diggings below the canyon. New claims were staked, shafts started, buildings erected, and businesses at Cameronton and Barkerville shortly opened their doors to customers.

Those miners who had remained for the winter were already taking out gold in the same comfortable amounts as in the past. John Cameron returned with two of his brothers, Roderick and Sandy, and he and his partners put the mine on a three-shift basis. Before long, Cameron was taking out anywhere from forty to over a hundred ounces of gold to each shift. In all, he sank three shafts. The last one, across the creek from his first, was the one that paid the richest dividends.

During the years 1863 and 1864 over a hundred companies staked claims from Richfield to Cameronton. Many of these were to continue in production until the end of the century, even though by far the greatest recovery of gold was taken during the first five years of production.

Some of these companies were represented by men from the Overlander Expedition. James Wattie, who had visited Williams Creek the autumn before, returned early in the spring of 1863 with his brother William. Together they located their claims downstream adjacent to that of John Cameron. The shaft they put down and the subsequent mining drift yielded gold to the amount of one hundred to one hundred and fifty ounces every twenty-four hours. Later they became associated with John Cameron, and between their own and the Cameron Company's claims, the two brothers amassed a great fortune.

One who was less fortunate than the Wattie brothers was A.L. Fortune, who had made the trip to Williams Creek in 1862. He couldn't make it to the mines until 1864 and then with but little capital. This fast disappeared and he was forced to borrow money in order to continue prospecting. Finally he left the Cariboo in the latter part of 1865, walking on foot from Barkerville to Quesnel, one of many who had not found his Eldorado.

Some examples of the large amounts of gold won by the successful companies on Williams Creek during the years 1862, '63 and '64 are: William Cunningham's Company in 1862 to '63 took out $270,000 from five hundred feet of gravels; in 1863 the Adams yielded $50,000 from fifty feet; the Steele, $120,000 from eighty feet; the Diller, located in 1862, had actually taken out one hundred and two pounds troy of gold in three days that year, $240,000 from fifty feet; the Burns, $140,000 from eighty feet; the Canadian $180,000 from one hundred and twenty feet; the Moffat, $90,000 from fifty feet; the Tinker, $120,000 from one hundred and forty feet; the Wattie, $130,000 from one hundred feet; the Wake-Up-Jake, reaching bedrock in 1864, yielded from a crevice $800 in gold in one pan! The Ericcson, which had been opened at Conklin Gulch, a stream flowing into Williams Creek, in 1863 produced fourteen hundred ounces of gold weekly during the mining season. The Prairie Flower, reaching pay in 1864, took out one hundred and seventy ounces of gold in one day. Gold at that time sold for $16 an ounce; troy weight is twelve ounces to the pound. These yields would turn the eyes of the world to Barkerville. Smaller scale successes were notable, too. Besides these few examples of flourishing mines there were hundreds of claims which, located on the fringes of the deep, rich channels of Williams Creek, yielded to their owners anywhere from $20 to $60 a day on the average.

The year 1863 was for most one of hard work with little of pleasure. All day long one could hear the sound of saws biting into wood, trees falling, water wheels creaking, the blacksmiths' hammers sharpening tools and the shouts of men at work echoed endlessly in the small valley. Numerous torches flickering above the shafts and reflecting on the silent spruce trees through the night presented a weird and wonderful picture to any who had the time to appreciate the wonder of what had happened to the primeval calm of this infinitely remote wilderness valley.

Countless cabins now were erected on the hillsides of the creek. By the end of the year over three thousand claims had been located. At the height of the mining season the population had risen to four thousand miners and businessmen. Winter would drive many to warmer climates, especially those with money to spend, but five hundred hardy ones had determined to stay and challenge the intense cold. Many mine owners planned to operate throughout the winter months. The recorded output of gold for the Cariboo then, in 1863, was $3,913,563.

In each of the next two years, 1864 and 1865, the output was officially given as near the four-million mark, but so much gold went out by private hand and was otherwise unreported that it has been estimated the yield actually was at least twice that recorded. Allan Francis, a United States representative in the year 1863, calculated that the figure for that year would have been nearer the six-million mark.

Although 1863 is referred to as Cariboo's banner year, large quantities of gold would continue to be mined for many years to come. Every once in a while, spectacular discoveries were made on a new creek or new ground of old claims. In 1865 great enthusiasm was created by the tremendous richness of the Ericcson claim, first discovered in 1863. This claim produced $168,000 in gold in seven weeks of mining in 1865. Across the creek and below the settlement of Cameronton a large number of claims located in 1863 and '64 paid good dividends. But the rich pay streak of a number of these was not discovered until sometime in the seventies. Examples of these are the Forest Rose, whose total output over the years was $430,000; the Aurora and also the Prince of Wales. This latter claim was not fully worked out even in the eighties. Its yield was $250,000 in all, over the years.

The total output of gold from Williams Creek and two of its tributaries, Conklin and Stout's Gulch, was estimated to be approximately $30,000,000 from 1861 to 1898. By far the greater portion of this, perhaps as much as two-thirds, was recovered during the sixties. Despite the fact of the much lower yields in subsequent years the miners never lost confidence that there was more gold still to be discovered. It was due in great part to their staunch confidence, enthusiasm and energies that the later discoveries were made.

But for all that the miners did feel a great deal of dissatisfaction in the government's treatment of them and believed that it was a deterrent to progress in the mining field. One thing they criticized hotly was the tax imposed on them for each ounce of gold they wrested from the gravels. They felt that the recording fees should have been all the government demanded, considering the onerous outlay of capital and labour they had to put at risk to make a paying mine.

As early as 1863 a petition signed by more than one hundred miners on Williams Creek was presented to the government, asking for an amendment in the mining act. They wanted, among other things, better assurance of holding the claims they staked, even if they were absent. This petition was signed by most of the owners of rich claims as well as many others. Such men as I.P. Diller, W.W. Cunningham, John Cameron, John R. Adams, Hardy M. Curry, David Grier, Peter C. Dunlavey, William Barker, J.C. Beedy, William Rankin, Thos. R. Pattullo, W.H. Steele and John Houser signed their names and the petition was presented to the Grand Jury, assembled at the courthouse on July 3, 1863. It was also suggested that a mining board be formed to protect the interests of the miners. This was later accomplished and a board containing twelve men was put in office. Some of the first members of this board were W.H. Steele, John Kurtz and W.W. Cunningham.

Whether as a result of the petition or not, in time an act was passed which enabled a miner, after he had worked on his claim for a period of five years and spent a prescribed amount of money on it, to obtain title by Crown grant. Thenceforth all he would need to do was pay land taxes on what were, in truth, real estate claims. In 1874 O.B. Travaillot, one of the first BC Land Surveyors in the district, arrived to survey the existing claims. By 1875 hundreds of claims in the Cariboo were duly measured and Crown granted by the government.

Long after the first discoverers had left the Cariboo or had passed away, men continued to press on into Williams Creek to try their luck in the goldfields. Many of these succeeded beyond their greatest hopes. Meanwhile it is interesting to note just what became of those first discoverers and some of the men who worked with such great success on the creek.

William (Bill) Dietz very early suffered poor health and was forced to return frequently to the coast. Although his claim is reported as only paying "good wages steadily," and he is often referred to as not having been as successful as the others in his mining, the total yield from the Dietz claim is recorded as $200,000—much more than some of the more widely publicized claims yielded. For all this, Dietz died at Victoria in 1877, in comparatively modest circumstances.

Edward Stout died in 1864, just two years after his discovery of gold below the canyon. He had never fully recovered his health after being wounded on his way to the goldfields. This, coupled with hard work and poor living conditions at the mines, contributed to his death. His company, The Wintrip, was carried on for many years after his death by his partner, Jack Wintrip. It is still known as the Wintrip Claim and is held today by the Lowhee Company.

Michael Burns and Vital La Force did exceptionally well on their claims at first; and in 1867 they went into the Omineca country where two of the creeks there are named "Burns" and "Vital" after them.

William Barker went to Victoria in the winter of 1862–63 and very shortly met and married Elizabeth Collyer, a widow from London. The next spring, he brought her back with him to the Cariboo. He spent money lavishly on his bride and also on any of his miner friends. Whenever he saw a prospector or a friend who needed help, he loaned or gave money away with an open hand. He was one who loved the atmosphere of a booming mining town and rejoiced that his own mine was a rich success. Almost every evening found him in one of the saloons buying the drinks and generally making merry.

There were ten partners in his mining company and the yield from their claims was $600,000. For the first few seasons things went very well, but gradually their claims began to yield less and less in gold, and eventually had become practically depleted.

At last Barker began to realize he was running out of both money and gold in the ground from which his money came. He attempted to collect sums owing him from the many he had befriended or grubstaked, but even this failed him. At length he was forced to take employment as a cook on the government road. Not too long after this he developed a cancer of the lip and was forced to quit work and return to Victoria. He lived from then on in straitened circumstances and eventually entered an "old man's home" at Victoria. He died there on July 11, 1894, thirty-two years almost to the month after he'd made the great strike on Williams Creek that would enrich so many.

Jack Wintrip—co-owner with Ned Stout of the Wintrip Claim on Stout's Gulch.

It can be said of Billy Barker that he was a man who stinted not when his mine was a humming success, and that for the few years this lasted he lived life to the fullest extent, not forgetting friends, nor those less fortunate than himself. In the town of Barkerville, named after him, his name is immortalized, and the memory of the man lingers as one who lived as miners liked to see it done by those who struck it rich.

When John Cameron returned from the East to Williams Creek in 1863, the fabulous output of gold from his mine earned him the title

"Cariboo" Cameron. In two short years he left for his home near Glengarry, and this time he took out with him such an immense fortune that he was able to give each of his five brothers a farm and a large sum of money. His brothers Dan, Sandy and Alex received in addition to a farm the sum of $20,000 each. To his brothers Roderick and Alan, who were with him for a short while, mining in Barkerville, he gave a farm apiece and something in the neighbourhood of $40,000.

John Cameron's nephew, James H. Cameron, in reminiscing about those early years, said he could vividly recall seeing some of the gold brought home by his uncle. "He kept a lot of his hoard in an old bureau drawer at home, and I remember the weight of the gold broke the bottom of the top drawer and crashed through the other drawers. I remember seeing nuggets as big as a teacup," he said. (These latter would have been retorted gold ingots.)

Besides securing the future of family and assisting many friends, Cameron also endowed Queen's University, Kingston, with a sum of money to be used in the education of the family descendants, this same nephew recalled.

It was shortly after his return to Cornwall, Ontario, that Cameron married another woman from home. This was Christianne (Christy) Adelaide Wood from nearby Osnabruck Corners. For her he built a beautiful home near Summertown. It was constructed of white marble at a cost of $60,000 and against his own inclinations became a showplace in the years that followed. In the corner of one beautiful stained-glass window Cameron had the year of the house's construction, 1865, blown into the glass. For him it was a happy 1865.

John Cameron had not been home too long when humiliating suspicion was cast upon him concerning his first wife, Sophia. For some reason a rumor spread that the body he'd brought back for burial was that of an Indigenous woman, and not his wife. Some claimed he had put gold in the coffin for safe transport. It wasn't until the body was exhumed that the gossip was stilled. From the dead woman's mother there came a cry of anguish as she recognized first her daughter's shawl and then her face and form.

The generous Cameron eventually lost most of his own fortune in unlucky investments in timber at Owen Sound and in a contract to build the Lachine Canal. With his second wife, Christy, he returned to Barkerville in 1888, hoping to make still a third fortune. But this time he was not successful, and he died at Barkerville on November 7th of that same year. They buried him in the little cemetery above Cameronton. It was the cemetery Cameron himself had started when he buried there one of his men, Peter Gibson, in the first years of mining. His wife lived in Vancouver for many years after his death, dying sometime in the 1920s.

James and William Wattie, associates of Cameron, both amassed fortunes from the gold of Williams Creek. In 1864 James left for his home in Huntingdon County, Quebec. For some years he operated a woollen mill which he later sold to the Montreal Cotton Company. He retired from business in 1890 and died in 1907. William Wattie returned home in 1865 and resumed his trade of machinist. He later became the superintendent of Knowles Loom Works, Worcester, Massachusetts. He invented and patented over sixty devices relating to weaving machinery. A prosperous world traveller, he revisited the Cariboo in 1893 in a sentimental journey to see again the region that had so favoured his career.

The Wattie claims continued to yield gold for some years after the brothers left.

This was true of many of the claims on Williams Creek. Long after the owners moved away or retired, gold was still recovered from their claims. Quite a number of those original mines were still operating profitably as late as 1898.

7
Lowhee, Grouse and Lightning Mines

Lowhee Creek was first discovered by Richard Willoughby in the summer of 1861. He had come into the province with the big rush on the Lower Fraser, and finally settled at Yale where he mined for some time. When news of the Cariboo gold reached Yale he left, working his way up the Fraser and at last to Antler and subsequently Richfield. He and his party, H. Tilton and two Patterson brothers, carried on from Richfield, passing the miners working the rich ground already staked. They followed Williams Creek down below the canyon and through the narrow valley where the famous deep diggings of Barker, Cameron and numerous others were yet to pour out their riches. Entering the flat, park-like ground through which Williams Creek meandered, they decided to traverse this and look for any other creeks that might exist below them. At last they came upon the lovely lake, later called Jack of Clubs Lake. Flowing from this was a pleasant stream which they named Willow River. Through a swamp which lay below the lake and subsequently into Willow River flowed another small stream. They could see from where they stood that it apparently coursed through a narrow ravine between two mountains—later Barkerville and Cow Mountains. This stream intrigued them as several pannings proved most interesting. They staked the ground, each having a claim, and Willoughby named his new mine after the miners' secret society at Yale to which he belonged, The Great Lowhee.

Although the ground was extremely shallow to bedrock, nowhere any deeper than four feet and sometimes but three feet, they didn't begin to mine at once. They had to make arrangements for supplies and also lumber for sluice boxes or tools to make the lumber.

However, when they did start, their success was quite sensational. In the short space of five weeks of mining, from late July to

September 8th, they took out $50,000 from four hundred feet of the creek. Willoughby and his partners returned to Yale early in September, each with ten to twelve thousand dollars in gold.

For the next two seasons they continued mining, then Richard Willoughby sold his interest. With the profits from his mining, which was said to be a considerable fortune, he took a homestead down in the Fraser flatlands near where the town of Chilliwack now stands. There are several Willoughbys in the area today, and some of these are more than likely his descendants.

As usual, word of the discovery travelled fast and soon there were numerous parties on the creek, staking and working claims. Before the first year was out, the entire length of the creek was staked, from its lower extremity near the site of the present town of Wells for a distance of two and a half miles through the mountains to its source. As mining progressed the ground became much deeper, necessitating drift mining. The water pressure here presented a serious problem. Nonetheless this was overcome, and almost the entire creek, except for a short distance in the upper part, was mined by drifting. This mining continued on into the seventies and eighties.

In the 1890s hydraulic mining began and would continue until 1964. Water for the hydraulicking was obtained from Ella Lake, a man-made lake near the head of Jack of Clubs Valley, and from Groundhog Basin at the foot of Mount Agnes. The water was carried by an extensive system of ditches about twenty-one miles in length. The ditches were seven feet wide, sloping to four feet at the bottom, and generally four and a half to five feet deep.

These ditches were dug by Chinese workers who also fell heir to the task of maintaining them. Small "ditch" cabins were built, each one being about eight miles from the other. Here the Chinese lived, each group attending his own section of ditch; maintaining a constant vigil lest it become blocked by slides, rocks or logs, and also tending the waste gates.

Until very recent years it was a familiar sight to see the Chinese miners starting out from Barkerville in early March with their supplies on large homemade hand sleds, each group bound for its own particular section. Their first task was to dig the snow from the ditches. Then they must repair any damage and strengthen any weak spot in the ditch and in the waste gate. Their work never ceased from March on to the end of the hydraulic season, sometime in late

October. On the ditch there was constant change and constant danger of change. The Chinese miners were faithful to their work and took pride in the excellent maintenance of these all-important ditches.

The Cariboo Consolidated Mining Company carried on hydraulicking on the creek for many years. Then, in the early part of the twentieth century, John Hopp began a program of consolidating these claims. He acquired one claim and then another until by 1906 he had not only the entire Lowhee Creek area but also claims on Stouts Gulch and Williams Creek. These extended for a distance of six miles to Mosquito Creek taking in part of the Willow River. He incorporated all these claims and placer leases into one company, The Lowhee Mining Company. This company has occasionally changed ownership, but it has remained in its operation and assets essentially as when incorporated. The distinction of being the first hydraulic manager of the company went to Laurent Muller.

Lowhee Creek at times and on some claims seemed as rich in gold as Williams Creek. There were many outstandingly rich claims, such as the Cornish Claim, the Sage Miller, Wyoming, the Black Bull and others. Watson's Gulch, a small tributary of Lowhee, was very rich, producing several hundred thousand dollars in gold.

Very early in its history a small settlement was established at the upper end of the creek on a large meadow forming the divide of Stouts Gulch and Lowhee Creek. This was Carnarvon, a little place scarcely known of today, but made up then of quite a number of cabins, a store or two, and a saloon. It served as a centre for the two hundred or so men working on the creek, as well as for those on Stouts Gulch.

Without doubt Lowhee is one of the most notable creeks in the Cariboo. Mining has been carried on here almost continually for over a hundred years. Here, as elsewhere, the production cannot be truly estimated, but the recorded output is said to be well over two and a half million dollars.

Richard Willoughby could not have dreamed of the immense wealth and long span of operation of his little Lowhee Creek when he first began mining in its shallow ground in July of 1861.

The history of Grouse Creek is a long and varied one. It was first discovered early in 1861 by a group of prospectors who decided to follow Antler Creek to its source. Leaving Discovery Rock they continued up the creek for a distance of about two miles where they came to an alpine meadow which formed itself into a beautiful level pass.

Continuing for a half mile or so, they came upon the headwaters of another creek which flowed in a northerly direction down a narrow ravine through heavy, coarse, broken boulders. Taking test pans as they made their way down the creek, they came to an outcrop of the bedrock just below a sharp bend in the creek. Here their results were more than encouraging and they staked a claim, the Discovery, on this new unexplored creek which was to become known as Grouse Creek. The men worked their claim for many years, taking out large amounts of gold.

The attention attracted by the richness of the Discovery Claim drew scores of prospectors into the area, who stayed a while then moved on, apparently unsuccessful, but who were constantly being replaced by others.

The most noteworthy claim, besides the Discovery, was the Texas which was located by a group of Americans above the Discovery. These men put in drifts to the right of the creek and found a section of the original creek bed. It paid them very well, but later they came upon the really rich section of the old channel to the left of the creek in comparatively shallow ground on a limestone dyke. From this they took out a fabulous amount of gold. An old-timer in Barkerville had the good fortune to have actually known these men and he related that when they pulled out they had four pack animals loaded with two hundred pounds of gold each!

A small settlement of cabins and stores grew up on the left side of Grouse Creek, on the hillside across the creek from the Discovery Claim. Later almost all of it was destroyed by fire. The miners called this small place by the dignified name of Grouse Creek City.

One of the many prospectors who explored Grouse Creek in 1861 was George Downey. He worked on a small tributary much farther up the creek from the Texas and above the sharp bend. He built a cabin there which stood for many years as one of the landmarks of the trail from Antler to Grouse Creek. He was not successful in his mining and shortly left for Williams Creek, and his was one of the early claims there. It had a recorded yield of $100,000.

Much later, Major Downey, as he was most frequently called, moved to the Barkerville area—lower down through the meadows for a distance of about three miles. Where Willoughby had continued left of Williams Creek, he turned right, travelling through a narrow pass. Here, about two miles through Downey Pass, he found rich pay.

He built a cabin there and worked for many years on his claim.

In 1864 an American by the name of Robert Heron began doing some exploration work about a half mile below the Discovery Claim. After considerable work and expense he and his party found a section of the original Grouse Creek channel, from which they took out over three hundred thousand dollars in gold. They had spent a little less than half of this to get into the ground; and believing that it was practically worked out, they sold their claims for a mere four thousand dollars.

The new owners formed the Heron Company and were prepared to do considerable exploration work, but shortly thereafter found rich gravels only a foot and a half deeper than Heron's workings. From this they took out eighty to one hundred ounces of gold a week all through the ensuing season.

Their amazing good fortune brought hundreds into the area, in search of other sections of this fabulously rich channel. It was, however, an elusive one and seemed to frequently break off and its lead to disappear. From that time to the present day, prospectors and mining companies have searched for, and sometimes found, other sections of what has become known as the Heron Channel.

When sections of it were discovered, they were so rich as to be breathtaking. The Heron, the Discovery and other claims yielded anywhere from fifteen to twenty thousand dollars to the share in 1866.

By 1867 there were thirty-five companies on Grouse Creek. There were the Full Rig Company which paid a dividend of $200 a share for one week's work, the rich Cornelian Claim, the fabulously rich Duxford Shaft, the Hard-Up Claim and the Ne'er-Do-Well. The Hard-Up was the only producing company which was below the Heron Claim.

In the year 1867 the Heron Company found a remarkably rich section of the channel. From the creek the men of this company ran a tunnel into what proved to be a section of the old creek bed. This was the Jimmy Allen tunnel, and Allen, the foreman, took out $750,000 of gold from four hundred feet of the channel! The rock channel was so narrow and steep-sided that an eight-foot cap reached from one rim to the other. The gold was found on a hardpan layer eighteen inches above bedrock, and at times yielded five hundred ounces to the set. After this the Heron was referred to as "one of the richest, if not the richest channel for its size in the Cariboo."

The Heron Claim was the site of the most contentious mining dispute in the Cariboo. It took place in 1867 and was known at that time as the Grouse Creek War.

The Heron Company had received a franchise to build a flume several hundred feet along the creek to pick up water from the creek and carry it past their workings, thus keeping the workings reasonably dry. This operation enabled them to work into the gutter of the creek, and they began to take out fifty to one hundred ounces of gold a day.

This obvious richness caused a big rush, and every foot of the creek was re-staked, the Canadian Company staking over the ground which the Heron Company had covered by franchise. Members of the Canadian Company had obtained from Judge Begbie the setting aside of any future appeal from the Gold Commissioner's Court. Then the Canadian Company proceeded to work the ground which they had staked.

The Heron Company took steps to have the trespassers moved from the disputed ground and were supported by the Gold Commissioner. The Canadian Company then found, to their sorrow, that no appeal existed for them, due to the court order they themselves had obtained from Judge Begbie. Nevertheless, they refused to withdraw, and when an order was made for their arrest, they resisted by force.

The Gold Commissioner, Henry M. Ball, now swore in some twenty or thirty special constables to enforce his order. The Canadian Company reciprocated by gathering together a force of about four hundred men and prepared to meet force with force. In the face of this threat, the Gold Commissioner found himself powerless.

After some further appeals, Henry Ball wired Governor Seymour for assistance. On July 19, 1867, personnel of the Canadian Company charged the personnel of the Heron Company and drove them by force not only from the disputed ground, but also from the heretofore undisputed ground the Heron Company was working. They took possession of the Heron Company's workings and commenced to take out quantities of gold, variously reported as from one hundred to one thousand ounces a day. They kept a large force at work and worked night and day, with the intention of having the ground worked out by the time the dispute was over. The Heron Company remained off their ground to await further developments, and at the end of three days the claim had lapsed. The Canadian Company now set up a

subsidiary company known as the Sparrowhawk and took possession of the remainder of the Heron ground.

Governor Seymour reached Richfield on August 7, 1867. He met
agents of the two warring camps and tried to induce the Canadian
Company to deliver the twelve feet of disputed ground to the government and to pay over to some public official the amount of gold tak-
en out. The officers of the Canadian Company were also instructed
to turn over to the authorities the members of their company who
had opposed the police. Eight men gave themselves up and were sen-
tenced to three months' imprisonment for opposing the authorities,
but the remaining members of the Canadian Company petitioned
throughout the area and had the sentences reduced to two days. Governor Seymour returned to the coast. He had failed to bring justice.
The law-abiding people of the Cariboo complained that the Governor
had only encouraged rowdyism and that he had sided with the rebels.

To answer the complaints and silence criticism, the Governor, after consulting with Chief Justice Needham, issued the latter a special
commission to hear and end the dispute. The Chief Justice, his son,
and the Honorable Chartres Brew, the latter relieving Henry Ball,
arrived at Richfield on September 15, 1867. The following day, the
court hearings were opened and the trial lasted for a lively ten days.
Chief Justice Needham returned the ground to the Heron Company,
along with the gold held in court, reported to have been to the value
of $3,600.

Of the many companies that were formed in an attempt to discover
a section of the rich Heron Channel, perhaps the most long-lived and
best known are the Hard-Up and the Waverly Mining Companies. The
Hard-Up Company, formed in 1867, had for its original members John
Bowron, Anthony MacAlindon, Joshua Spencer Thompson, Guy Land-
er Shephard and David Robertson. These men sank deep shafts downstream from the Heron Claim and came upon a channel which carried
gold, though the recovery was never as great as that of the Heron.

The Talisman and Princess Marie Companies in 1867 explored
ground about a half mile below the Heron Claim. Here they put down
shafts of the same name, and also another, the Lady of the Lake, all
named from Sir Walter Scott's Waverley novels. Some drifting was
done, but difficulty in handling the water forced them to suspend
operations. These claims, as well as those of the Hard-Up Company,
were Crown granted in 1875.

Hydraulic mining on Lowhee Creek. Note the posts from early drift mining exposed by this operation. Courtesy J.J. Gunn

In 1879 the Waverly Hydraulic Mining Company acquired these claims. It is interesting to note how the ground was first opened up. The directors believed that an open cut could be put through to the bottom of the Talisman Shaft, where they wished to start working, but in attempting this they came upon a heavy rock rim. Consequently they were forced to put a drift through this rim—work which took them three years. In 1882 they put a flume and riffle blocks in the drift, diverted Grouse Creek down the shaft and from this point carried out their hydraulic mining. Several million yards of material was worked out through this drift which now became a tunnel.

The Waverly Hydraulic Mining Company continued up until 1919. In the ledger of this company appear such names as I.B. Nason, Joe Mason, Andrew Kelly, John Pomeroy, William Renni, James and John Bibby and many others, all of whom at one time or another were directors of the company. The first chairman of the company was William Renni.

For all their long years of endeavor it was not until 1896 that they were able to pay a dividend of one dollar a share. For the next several years they paid dividends, some as high as four and five dollars a share.

·Interest in the Crown grant claims and leases they later acquired has never wavered. The New Waverly Hydraulic Mining Company was formed in 1919, with C.W. Moore as manager. In 1933 the Barkerville Gold Mines Company bought out this company and it carried on under Moore's management until in 1948 Antler Mountain Gold bought out the assets.

Lowhee Creek. Piping out the gutter with the No. 6 monitor, October 1922. Courtesy J.J. Gunn

The Hard-Up Company's assets were acquired in 1904 by the United Mining Company which took out, from what proved to be a lower extension of the original Heron Channel, enough gold to pay seventy thousand dollars to each of the three shareholders. The three members were John Bowron, Beech LaSalle and Joseph Wendle. After this no further work was done on this claim by them, but at a later date Joe Wendle sold his one-third interest to the Barkerville Gold Mines and also acquired shares in that company.

The Princess Marie, Talisman and Hard-Up Claims, first Crown granted in 1875, as this is written, are still held in good standing by the Antler Mountain Gold Company.

The estimated total output of gold from Grouse Creek is close to four million dollars.

From the year 1864 on, the creek was alive with prospectors, miners and mining companies. Grouse Creek City for a time flourished, until destroyed. A half mile below it, Grouse Town grew up on the banks of the creek near the site of the Heron workings. Stores, boarding houses, saloons, blacksmith shops, a dance hall and other businesses did a roaring business for ten to fifteen years. When the cattle drives arrived in Barkerville the traders and merchants on Grouse Creek always bought twenty to thirty head and ranged them on the meadowland a half mile below the Heron Claim. This meadow

Panning clean-up. Joe House, son of one of the very early prospectors of Williams Creek. Courtesy R. McDougall

was enclosed with a pole fence for the purpose. Many of the entertainers who arrived at Barkerville also made arrangements to entertain at Grouse Town. Anthony MacAlindon had a store, saloon and dance hall. This store was still operating until the late 1880s. Louie Wing had a prosperous business at Grouse Town as a prominent merchant and trader.

Besides Grouse Town there was another settlement at Boone Sawmill above the Discovery Claim.

In the old ledger from the MacAlindon's store and saloon appears the record of many of the men who were working on Grouse Creek over the years. Here are to be found such names as Stevenson, Jimmy Allen, Joe Mason, Major Downey, Guyet, Pat Carey and Pat Howley.

Stevenson, one of the shareholders of the Heron Company, died and left his widow his share of the gold taken from the Heron channel. She invested $35,000 of this in shares of the first BC Electric Company.

Guyet, the finder of a little creek running parallel to Grouse, took out a good deal of gold there. Then, many years later he said to his partner as they stood where he'd found the first gold, "If my theory about this creek is right, then the channel should run from here across Antler Creek and there should be a section of it right on that ledge." They investigated, and at the very spot that he'd pointed out, they found a rich continuation of the Guyet Channel. The Guyet Mining Company, which he subsequently formed, continued mining and exploration work on this bench for the next sixteen years but took out large quantities of gold only in the first two years.

Two of the shareholders of the Guyet Company were Pat Carey and Pat Howley. These men also did a great deal of prospecting in and around the area of Grouse Creek; Carey Creek and Mount Howley bear their names.

Joe Mason was a shareholder of the Heron Company. He was one of the district's outstanding merchants and cattle buyers, with a store at Barkerville and later a dairy some three miles away at Pleasant Valley.

In MacAlindon's account book these names and many others appear, bringing alive the exciting years on Grouse Creek. Alongside the names are such items as drinks, 50¢; a bottle of brandy, $2.70; cigars (spelled segars); oysters, etc. Then in another ledger appear the accounts paid, marked thus: "Paid in dust $39.75."

The Heron Channel and the possibility of a section of it still remaining keeps Grouse Creek an area of interest. By no means has exploration of this creek exhausted its possibilities.

Gold was discovered on Lightning Creek by Ned Campbell and his partners in July 1861. It was incredibly rich, second only to Williams Creek in gold production. Its history and that of the two towns, Van Winkle and Stanley, that grew up on its banks are fully as stirring as that of Williams Creek.

It is related that Ned Campbell and his companions had a most hazardous trip as they followed the creek from where it rose about three miles west and below Bald Mountain Plateau, down the steep ravines and sheer drops to Spruce Canyon, about seven miles below. It was made during the high-water season, when any little rivulet or stream became a roaring freshet, dislodging huge boulders and great sections of earth which often caused a thunderous avalanche of rocks, clay and rubble to flash past them, splattering their passage with almost impassable debris. When they finally arrived at the canyon in a torrential rainstorm they were exhausted from their frightening descent. Some say that the name Lightning was given the creek because of the storm that beset this trip. But others maintain that Bill Cunningham, Jack Hume and Jim Bell had discovered and named the creek earlier in 1861.

It was on the lower part of Spruce Canyon that gold was discovered by Campbell and his partners, and they began making preparations to sink a shaft. The bedrock was at first only from eight to thirty feet below the surface; but from the outset they had trouble with "slum," a fine, wet silt that is heavy and gummy to handle. This caused them numerous heartbreaking setbacks, but the results of their labours more than offset this when finally they reached the pay in early October. In their first three days of mining, they took out seventeen hundred ounces of gold! Although their claims did not continue to be that rich, in three months' work the gold output was two hundred thousand dollars.

Very shortly numerous claims were staked both on Lightning Creek and on many small tributaries. One of the most successful of these was Van Winkle Creek, named by its discoverer for a river bar near Lytton that had been highly successful. Over two thousand feet at the lower end of Van Winkle Creek yielded anywhere from one hundred to two hundred and fifty dollars a day per man throughout its first season.

Another tributary, Last Chance Creek, on the south side of Lightning and about a mile below Van Winkle, was discovered in 1861 by a man named Donavan and his partner. They were on their way out of the Cariboo, broke and disillusioned, when they decided to take one last chance. They found pay near the surface which encouraged them to sink an eighty-foot shaft. Their Discovery Claim took out forty pounds of gold in one day! From a half mile of this creek the recorded yield was $250,000 in that one season.

The Butcher Bench, one of the richest of all the claims discovered on Lightning or its tributaries, was found by Joseph Gilmour on November 4, 1863. This was on a bench sixty feet above the creek bed and was so named because the actual discovery of gold was made by easing a butcher knife into a crevice of the bedrock. One of the largest nuggets taken from the Cariboo was from this claim. It weighed slightly over thirty-six ounces. The gold output in one area of only a few yards was said to be $122,000.

Despite the auspicious first season, none of the following years was anywhere near as successful on Lightning Creek. The bedrock was extremely deep, being from eighty to one hundred and fifty feet below the surface, and water and slum conditions made mining almost impossible. After a couple of seasons of work the creek was practically abandoned at the end of 1864.

However, by 1870 many of the earlier claims resumed work on the creek and its various tributaries. A costly bedrock drain, seventeen hundred feet in length, was put in by the Van Winkle Company. Besides this, the water was finally brought under control by a co-operative method of the miners. They powered pumps draining water from the shafts by use of twelve water wheels all running simultaneously. The total amount of water being pumped was approximately fourteen thousand gallons a minute, or twenty million gallons a day.

As a result of all this, old companies began working and new locations were opened up for a distance of two miles along the creek. Such companies as the Vancouver, Victoria, The Point, Van Winkle, Vulcan and others began paying big dividends per share. The Vancouver with thirteen interests, paid $21,000 to the share. Others were the Victoria with sixteen interests, $80,000 to the share; The Point with six interests, $13,000 to the share. The Van Winkle is said to have paid even larger dividends, despite its earlier expense with the bedrock drain. The Vulcan with ten interests paid $10,000 to the share.

Two thriving towns were created by the tremendous success of Lightning Creek. These were Van Winkle and Stanley. The combined population of the two at the height of the mining operations was in the neighbourhood of five thousand people. There was the usual quota of hotels, stores, blacksmith shops, saloons, dance halls and other businesses. One hotel, The Lightning, still standing, was originally built at Richfield and moved to Stanley. Several additions have been added to it over the years.

For a long time the government post office was at Van Winkle, and even when moved to Stanley it was still called the Van Winkle post office.

In the 1930s there were about two hundred people at Stanley, and two hotels were still operating and continued to remain open until 1947, when one of them, the King George Hotel, burned down. Jimmy Williams and his wife operated the Lightning Hotel. The meals they offered the traveller and their hospitality can never be forgotten by any who stayed there. Mrs. Williams put in a long, hard day at the hotel.

She did the cooking, and she carried all the water for the hotel from a barrel in the creek which was protected by a small shed. She made the weary traveller welcome, seeming to realize his needs. From both her husband and herself emanated a heartwarming welcome. After her death during World War II, Jimmy Williams continued to operate the hotel for some time, but finally gave it up. He prospected in the area for many years and was still at it till shortly before his death in 1960.

A number of well-known men who had arrived in the last century were still living in or near Stanley in the thirties. Harry Jones was one who came to Lightning Creek in 1863 and lived there until shortly before his death at ninety-seven years of age. During that time, he made two fortunes from his mining. For some years he was a member of the British Columbia Legislature, representing the Cariboo riding. He died at Victoria in 1936 and was buried there. But, in accordance with the conditions of his will, his body was later exhumed and brought to Stanley for burial. Harry Jones could not imagine anywhere but the Cariboo as his final resting place.

His partner, Captain John Evans, had led a party of twenty-six Welshmen into the Cariboo in the early sixties. He, too, later represented the Cariboo in the legislature. He was an extremely well-liked man, of the old school, with sterling qualities and rugged courage.

George Shaw, a man of kindly disposition and a happy outlook, lived and prospected at Lightning Creek for his lifetime. His father had taken out over $65,000 from Hardscrabble Creek, a tributary of the Willow River, in the sixties and later made Stanley his headquarters. George had been one of the first babies born at Lightning Creek. For many seasons he prospected in an attempt to discover the continuation of his father's lead, and although he was unsuccessful in this, he enjoyed his life and work.

Sam Montgomery prospected and mined on Lightning Creek in both the nineteenth and twentieth centuries. He was in charge of the Vancouver Company's workings. When this ground was worked out, he uncovered a ledge of rotten quartz from which he took six hundred ounces of gold. The rich ledge is now called the Montgomery Ledge, after him. When he was eighty years old he began a shaft on the north side of Lightning Creek and developed the Point Claim. At a depth of sixty feet he sent up his first pay dirt, which was fifty ounces in one pan! Some of the nuggets in this pan were as large as fair-sized potatoes, according to Harry Edens, who worked for him at that time. An estimate of $250,000 is attributed to this claim.

William Houseman was a most colourful character who arrived on the Creek in 1870. He was known as "The Duke of York," and was by no means admirable. He was six feet eight inches in height and had a fine, distinguished appearance.

When he first came to Lightning Creek in 1870, he opened a butcher shop which thrived. Later he opened a hotel at Van Winkle which was halfway between the mining operations then going on and Stanley. This was called the "New Drop Inn." Here he charged the miners nothing for room and board but made up for this by really gaining from his entertainment and drinks. It is said that in a large drum heater he placed only a lighted candle behind a red-coloured paper, which, shining through the mica-fronted stove gave the appearance of warmth. Hot drinks were given to any newcomer on his arrival and soon the need of other heat was not felt, or such was Houseman's theory.

He made a fortune in the Cariboo and left for the coast. However, it was not long before he had spent this, and he returned in the hope of making another. He was unsuccessful and finally went to Victoria where he died in 1922. He is remembered chiefly in the Cariboo for his eccentricities and for his many wildcat schemes for making money.

The total output of Lightning Creek is estimated at twelve to thirteen million dollars. No accurate record was kept, and miners believe this to be a truer estimate than the recorded five to six million.

Several sections of the creek have never been bottomed, and it is held by many miners that the bedrock here would still yield the fabulous amounts of the sixties and seventies. In all the Cariboo, slum and water have been the greatest obstacle to success, and on Lightning Creek and its tributaries this was truer than elsewhere.

8
WILLIAMS CREEK IN 1863

The little towns and settlements followed almost in the footsteps of the miners. Their shaft houses, cabins and small buildings for storing supplies were the nucleus of these places. The miners themselves might be said to have been the first merchants on the creeks, inasmuch as they very often had a contract with the pack trains coming into the camps and, even though the supplies were for their own use, they were able at times to supply or sell some of their stock to those in need.

By the month of July 1861, four hundred and eight pack animals laden with supplies arrived in the town of Antler. These comprised about ten to fifteen separate pack trains, some for Antler, others on their way to the new mines farther on. It is said of Lightning Creek that the pack trains arrived two weeks after the first strike.

At Williams Creek the pack train of A.G. Norris arrived in the early part of August 1861. This was the first lot of supplies to reach the creek by pack animal, all others having been brought on the backs of the miners themselves or by men hired for the purpose of packing. At this same time J.C. Beedy was one of the men recorded to have made his way over to Williams Creek to make preparations for opening a small supply base there.

By mid-March the following year, the construction of twenty business buildings had already been started, and less than six weeks later some of these were able to sell meals and liquor and to rent rooms. However, the great shortage of supplies, already noted, forced them to close their doors till the end of June 1862.

The following three months of July, August and September found Williams Creek doing a brisk business not only at Richfield but to a lesser extent, at Cameronton by September.

The Victoria *Colonist* had many interesting items of news about the mines in the Cariboo and their September 10th issue gives us some idea of the activity on the creek during the summer of 1862.

The following are concerned with Williams Creek and are herein quoted verbatim:

> Steele's, Abbot's and the other mines are still as rich as ever.
>
> Mr. J. T. Scott and Cameron of New Westminster have "struck it rich" on Williams Creek, about a half mile above the town. The diggings are three-quarters of a mile above any other rich ground.
>
> John Emmory, a miner, died in Cameron's New Saloon on August 19th, of pleurisy. He had been ill for six weeks, and was attended by his brother in his dying moments.
>
> An unknown man fell from a platform on Sunday evening in front of Smith's store. This was on August 16th. He fell twelve feet and died of a broken neck.
>
> There are two respectable married ladies on the creek. Two billiard tables have been brought to the creek and set up in a saloon at $1 a game. [This last item was printed all in one paragraph!]
>
> A notice prohibiting gambling under a penalty of $100 was stuck up by Commissioner Elwyn, but the games go on openly as before.
>
> The weather is execrable, raining and hailing. One hailstone measured on July 22nd was one and-a-half inches in diameter.

The item about the gold strike leads one to wonder if John Cameron might have discovered his gold simultaneously with William Barker, or even earlier. Several facts support this theory: There were *no* claims three quarters of a mile above the rich ground on Williams Creek, and a half mile above the town is McCallum's Gulch. There was a J.H. Scott who was later a prominent merchant in Cameronton. John Cameron was a veteran of the Fraser River Gold Rush, and at one time had his centre at New Westminster.

John Emmory had discovered gold on Emmory Gulch, a tributary of Stouts Gulch. His brother carried on mining at this rich gulch for some years afterwards.

On September 12th, 1862 these interesting items appeared in the *Colonist:*

Thorp, a butcher, went broke giving credit.

Major Downey's claim is paying sixteen to twenty-four ounces a day. A beautiful gold-quartz nugget valued at $104 was found on this claim about three weeks ago.

Besides these pieces of news there was a "Letter from Antler," written on September 2nd, by E. Brigand. It was mentioned that the Bishop of BC was on Williams Creek. Most of these news items dealt with occurrences of as much as a month before time of publishing.

By July 1862, Father Charles Grandidier arrived at Richfield and held services there for those of Roman Catholic faith. The next month Reverend James Sheepshanks arrived and for the next two months came over each Sunday from Antler to hold services for the Church of England.

As yet no church was built, but plans were underway by both Roman Catholic and English Church representatives to build, rent or purchase a place of worship.

In 1863 the population of Williams Creek rose by leaps and bounds and was to reach a peak of four thousand by mid-summer. Very soon clean domestic water was supplied to the towns from tanks dug in the hillside and cribbed. In time three main flumes were to run over the tops of buildings and the street of Barkerville into barrels and troughs.

During the early spring of 1863 there were a number of cases of typhoid fever in several Cariboo towns and on Williams Creek itself, where a few men died of the disease. This, coupled with the occasional appearance of scurvy and other illnesses and accidents in the mines, led the miners to hold a meeting where it was decided to petition the government for a hospital. At the second Grand Jury, held in July, their petition was presented to presiding Judge Begbie. The result was a small contribution from the government. Most of the money was raised by public subscription among the miners. On August 24th the log hospital building was started. It consisted of one ward, doctor's office and kitchen, and was completed and officially opened in October 1863.

The hospital was erected at a little settlement called Marysville, which was slightly below and across the creek from Cameronton.

The Royal Cariboo Hospital situated above Cameronton, taken in the thirties. The original hospital was at Marysville.

Marysville, built on the bench land above the creek, was a small town which for a time enjoyed great importance. The rich Forest Rose and Californian claims were close by, and a large number of residences. Adam's Sawmill was there. There was even, at one time, a hotel, the Bowden, which shared with the new hospital the neighbourliness of Marysville. As the years went by and the miners' claims were worked out, the settlement was gradually deserted by White miners. The Chinese then took over, and still later Indigenous people found a use for the free shelters.

The first doctor at the hospital was Dr. A.W.S. Black, who had spent many years in the Australian gold mining fields and consequently was on familiar ground. He very shortly received as guests the eminent Dr. Cheadle and his companion Lord Milton. Dr. Cheadle later wrote glowingly of this visit to the hospital, and of the warmth of the hospitality received there. After beginning with, "We were royally entertained by the doctor and staff of the Royal Cariboo Hospital at Marysville," he went on to describe a wonderful evening. Toward the end of the evening the orderly of the hospital became so tipsy that they had some difficulty steering him across the high, narrow Williams Creek bridge to his cabin at Cameronton. (The posts of this same bridge that spanned the creek from Marysville to Cameronton have recently been exposed and can be seen today.)

The hospital, most often referred to as Williams Creek Hospital, remained at Maryvsille until 1891 when a building was erected on a new site above and slightly south of Cameronton. It was the only hospital in the Cariboo for more than forty years.

A mild joke connected with two men confined there has now become one of the stories of the Cariboo. They were the surveyor O.G. Travaillot and J.B. Malanion. Both men lay seriously ill and dying but they made light of it, and the legend has passed into posterity that they made a wager with one another as to which one would die first! As to which was the "winner," the record does not say. Malanion was an excellent violinist who was said to have played in the opera houses of Europe. He taught music to many of the children on Williams Creek.

In January of 1863 Thomas Elwyn asked to be relieved of his duties, and his place as Gold Commissioner was taken by Peter O'Reilly. The latter was a wonderful personality and had an innate understanding of and sympathy with the miners, with whom he was immensely popular.

Meanwhile, Thomas Elwyn, who couldn't help but become interested in the mining going on all around him, for a time himself went mining. In fact, he had given this as one of the reasons for resigning as Gold Commissioner, thinking it not right to become active in mining while employed as a public servant of the government. However, his venture did not turn out successfully.

Elwyn later joined the Gold Escorts, an organization instituted by the government to carry the heavy loads of gold out of the Cariboo for a fee set as a small percentage of the weight of gold thus moved and guarded. However, since the government did not guarantee safe delivery, few men bothered to use the service, preferring to take their own risks with their own gold. As a result, the Gold Escorts service failed miserably, and had it not been that Thomas Elwyn was a trusted and respected man, the small amount that was entrusted to the government gold escort system would in all likelihood have been considerably less. The plan was discontinued at the end of 1863.

The summer of 1863 was the occasion of long remembered excitement on the creek when a troupe of female German dancers were invited to perform at one of the saloons. They had originally been brought to California from Europe to entertain and dance with the miners. They were vivacious, many of them pretty, eager to please, with pleasant personalities. Many tributes to their high moral characters are to be found in records of the time. They were engaged by James Loring of the Diller, Loring and Hard Curry Company. At the same time, Loring purchased a French upright piano at Victoria to supply music for the dancing. This piano was shipped as far as Quesnel and from there four men carried it in its crate the sixty miles to Barkerville.

The Hurdy Gurdies, as these dancers were called (after the musical instruments to whose strains they danced), were immediately popular and became an institution on the creek, returning year after year. Many remained at Barkerville, marrying their miner friends who predictably fell in love with their stalwart charms.

Some time after their arrival on the scene, the Hurdy Gurdies were placed in the care of Fanny Bendixon, who had sold her hotel at Victoria and had come by way of Antler to Williams Creek. It is reported that she was the only woman who had packed her own personal belongings on her back from Antler to Barkerville. Madame Bendixon, as she was most frequently called, was a good-looking woman of an imposing build. With her dark hair piled high on her head, she presented a figure of dignity and composure. For all her quiet nature, the girls found in her a vigorous friend, defender and ally.

There were a few married women at Williams Creek in '63. Some of these were women whom the British Columbia Emigration Society, formed in 1862, had encouraged to come to the Vancouver Island colony from England. Most of the women who came on the first trip in 1862 were from English orphanages and had entered domestic service in the lower country. In September 1862 another group of sixty arrived at Victoria, almost half of whom married soon afterwards, some of them to Cariboo miners.

What with the dances and music and a few married women here and there on the creek, the towns took on a different atmosphere. Quite frequently one might hear a lively tune coming from a miner's cabin as he played his violin when his hard day's work was done. Violins were the favourite instruments on the creek, and many were the miners who owned one. Occasionally a plaintive song fell on the evening air, as one or another miner recalled the melodies of his homeland.

There were so many nationalities represented on Williams Creek that it became known as the "Valley of Flags." Each business-man flew the flag of his own country. There were flags of Great Britain, France, Italy, Holland, Denmark, Sweden, United States, Mexico, Germany and many more.

In August 1863 Peter O'Reilly posted notices of a public auction to sell lots in Barkerville at $200 each. The small mining camp was rapidly becoming a prosperous centre, along with its neighbour Cameronton.

The business of Cameron's Hotel & Saloon, the first hotel on Williams Creek, was eventually moved to Cameronton as the Pioneer Hotel by its owner, a Mrs. Cameron, not to be confused with Mrs. John A. One of the first businesses at Barkerville was that of W. Winnard, blacksmith and machinist. The Wake-Up-Jake bakery, owned by Andrew Kelly, was an early business there, as was the J.H. Scott store, already mentioned, at Cameronton.

Many of the thousands of cabins and also business buildings that were erected in 1862 and 1863 were built before the first sawmill was established by Meacham & Nason at Richfield in the summer of 1863. All of these buildings were made of logs, following the methods used by the first miners at Alexandria House, Quesnel Forks and Keithley. The only tools used for these first log buildings were an axe, two augers (a one-inch and a one-and-a-half-inch) and occasionally a two-inch wood chisel. (The augers had many other uses. Often they were used to make riffles in sluice boxes. Lines of holes which were two inches apart and spaced at two-inch intervals were drilled across the split timber that formed the second floor of the sluice box. The holes were staggered to prevent the wood from splitting between the holes and to provide effective retention of gold.)

The first cabins are easily identified by the type of construction, as no nails of any kind were available to the builders. The logs used in constructing the walls of the cabins were "saddled" at the corners; that is, they were cut to fit snugly together. In the earliest cabins, a "square-cut" method of saddling was used; in later cabins, or in buildings of a more permanent nature, a more elaborate type of saddling, the "dove-tail" method, was common. The logs used in the gables were held together by wooden dowels. A hole was bored through a log and into the log below with an auger, and a dowel was driven through to pin the logs together.

When the logs reached the height of the door the larger auger was used to bore a hole into the bottom log and one into the top log before it was put in place. These holes were at the extreme right or left of the door sills. A small pole was shaped and set in the hole in the sill and the top log put in place, the pole fitting into the hole in the log at the door head and jam. This log was firmly held by several dowels, and the pole then served as hinges for the door, the door being mortised and pinned to the pole.

In the opposite end of the cabin a hole was left in the wall from the floor up. It was generally four feet high and about five feet wide. In this space the fireplace was built with clay and boulders, with the chimney laid up past the roof on the outside of the cabin. The fireplace served for both cooking and for supplying heat, and in winter evenings provided light by which to read.

The roof consisted of poles about five inches thick. They were split and laid in two layers. In the first layer the round side was turned down, and in the second layer it was turned up, with each pole overlapping half of the pole beneath.

The cabin was then chinked with moss and sometimes with clay throughout.

The remnants of many such cabins can still be found from Marysville to Richfield, on Williams Creek, as well as on countless other creeks in the Cariboo.

9
THE ROAD TO THE MINES

It was the thousands of gold seekers following the new discoveries who were instrumental in the opening up of roads throughout the vast area of British Columbia, most of which had been accessible only by water or by following the trails of Indigenous people on foot, horse or mule.

In fact, the need of roads to the goldfields, and the subsequent building of them did much to prevent the political disruption of the western part of British North America. The forty-ninth parallel itself was in some dispute as hundreds of men arrived daily from the United States. Though many came by steamboat from San Francisco to Victoria and thence to Yale, a large percentage came also via Fort Colville in the United States through the Okanagan Valley to Kamloops and so north to the Cariboo. A good deal of the gold went out of the country unofficially by this latter route.

Governor Douglas was constantly being informed of this condition by the gold commissioners and other officials in his employ. The fact that he saw the need and instigated the building of the Cariboo Road, thus establishing it as the main line to the goldfields, was a great factor in firmly establishing British law and justice in the colony.

An interesting story that pointed up this need is connected with the racetrack built a few miles out of Antler near the creek which thenceforth bore the name Race Track Creek.

A group of miners at Antler, grown rich overnight, decided to bring some racehorses into the town. They ordered them shipped in from England, and the horses arrived in Victoria in 1861. Some effort was made to retain them on the coast, and Hastings was chosen for the races. But on further considering the facts, it was seen that it would have taken too long to obtain the necessary permission from the owners at Antler. So, reluctantly, the lovely animals were sent on up the Cariboo Trail with the idea that those interested could, if they wished, follow and attend the races. Several enthusiasts actually did follow the horses and attended the first meet.

The racetrack is visible to this day. It is about fourteen miles by road from Barkerville. Though not easily accessible, as the last two or three miles have to be taken on foot over a rough trail, still to those who have reached it and walked over the dim outline still evident in the flat grassy space, there has come a strengthened appreciation of those now distant days.

The track was a four-furlong straight course. The stones from the surface were piled along each side of the straight-away. At the finishing end of the course are the remains of the "Casino," a building which was approximately thirty by forty feet in size. The stone piles of two large fireplaces remain. It is understood to have been a two-storey building, with a bar-room and other amenities. The pack trail from the old town of Antler to Richfield passed close by. On the bench to the right of the track lie two unmarked graves. In the 1930s a white picket fence enclosed the graves; today only a few pickets remain. The graves, easily seen, do not suggest the length of time (over a hundred years) that has elapsed since they were dug.

One of the old-timers of Williams Creek, Johnny Houser, recalled his father telling how he and his friends went over to the Antler race track to attend the races, which were held from the first day of July until Labour Day. Long after this track fell into disuse the custom of holding horse races was one of the features of any holiday weekend, the races being run down the long street of Barkerville.

Sir James Douglas was one of the dignitaries who once attended the early races held at this track in the wilderness. It was during this trip that the Governor saw for himself the tremendous wealth that was being taken from the country, of which only a small portion was reaching the treasury in Victoria. He knew something must be done. On his return to Victoria he immediately embarked upon a firm road construction policy, which included the completion of the Dewdney Trail from Fort Hope to Fort Steele. This trail was to serve two purposes: first, as a tentative International Boundary, and second, as a pack trail to the coast.

In 1861 one of the greatest of road builders, Gustavus Blin Wright, had extended the Harrison-Lillooet road as far as Clinton, and in 1862 he was given a contract to complete it to the Cariboo. By the end of July 1863, he finished the road as far as Soda Creek. From there supplies and passengers travelled by steamboat the fifty miles to Quesnel (then Quesnelle Mouth).

The first boat used for the purpose was built during the winter of 1862 and was launched in May 1863. The boiler for this vessel, the *Enterprise,* was brought to Soda Creek in the form of steel sheets, or as we would say today, it was "prefabricated." Boiler-makers were not common but the blacksmiths of those days were very able men. They assembled the boiler and installed it in the *Enterprise,* which continued for many years to ply the river between Soda Creek and north of Quesnel to Fort George, and later to the upper Fraser and Nechako Rivers.

Two contractors, Thomas Spence and Joseph Trutch, in 1862 had completed Governor Douglas's Cariboo Road through the Fraser Canyon as far as Boston Bar, except for a short section that required heavy blasting to get rid of rock ridges.

In 1863 the Royal Engineers under Lieutenant Palmer built a nine-mile section of this road, and the rest of the distance to Clinton was completed by William Hood of Cache Creek. Hood's section of the road was said to be the best in the colony.

By early fall of 1863 the Cariboo Road was ready for traffic as far as Clinton where it joined the extended Harrison-Lillooet Road, and these two became one.

There was a good deal of rivalry between the two routes to the Cariboo after this, and for at least two years both were used extensively. Gradually, however, the Fraser Canyon route got the lead and was being used almost exclusively by the end of the sixties.

These roads made a tremendous difference to the miners. It was now possible to get to the mines much more quickly, and supplies which heretofore had come by pack train now were brought in by freight wagon in larger amounts, at lower cost and in much better condition on arrival. Freight rates dropped from seventy-five cents a pound to fifteen cents.

Although the tolls placed on the roads by Governor Douglas to help pay for their cost were said to offset this reduction, still the prices of equipment and provisions took a noticeable drop in the summer of 1863. Such items as flour, which had been $1.00 to $1.25 a pound, was now 32¢ to 35¢; and butter which had been $2.50 was $1.25. Everything was down proportionately. Tea was $1.25, coffee $1.00, bacon 50¢ to 75¢, and sugar 50¢ to 60¢ a pound each. The shortages that had

The river boat from Soda Creek to Quesnel and Fort George.

been experienced in the Cariboo the year before were not repeated, and life took on a much pleasanter and more comfortable prospect.

By 1864 the construction of the last phase of the Cariboo Road began. This was from Quesnel to Williams Creek, a distance of nearly sixty miles. Gustavus Wright had the contract to build the first part of this, from Quesnel to Cottonwood, some twenty miles. A trail had already been cut out over the route in 1862 by a Mr. Kyse. This trail was to have been four feet in width, but Thomas Elwyn, in a report to the government, said at that time that Kyse had made an excellent job of this and that he had over-extended himself by making it eight feet in width and had also constructed eight bridges. This was in June 1862, and he mentioned that two or three horses had already gone over this line and that it was reported that a drove of cattle and three pack trains had reached Cottonwood, at that date. This route was better than the Keithley-Antler-Richfield trail and hundreds of prospectors used it. It offered much more grazing for the horses and was altogether an easier trail.

By the end of September 1864, Gustavus Wright completed the wagon road to Cottonwood. The remainder of the road from Cottonwood to Barkerville was completed by late fall of 1865 by a Mr. Munro.

When the first stagecoach finally reached Williams Creek on the completed Cariboo Road, the travel situation was tremendously eased; there was great rejoicing, not only by the people in the Cariboo but also by the many in the South who now were assured of transportation. After this, many of the miners' wives, for the first time, reached the scene of their husbands' work, and many more women arrived at Williams Creek for visits or even to open businesses.

The Cariboo Road when completed was a source of wonder and admiration to the many who visited British Columbia. It stretched for a distance of nearly four hundred miles from Yale at the head of navigation in the lower Fraser River to the mines on Williams Creek and was built by the infant colony of British Columbia in less than three years. To help pay for its construction, Governor Douglas had placed tolls on the road for varying periods of from five to seven years, so that no future generation would be charged for this mammoth task. The road was narrow and winding, and particularly through the treacherous Fraser and Thompson River canyons, it had to be built in many places on immense masonry fills, or gigantic cribwork. When completed it supported long lines of pack animals, heavy freight wagons and six or eight-horse coaches. Not until the next century was this pioneering highway to be straightened out and widened and made into the magnificent scenic motor route it is today.

10
Pushing Back the Frontier

The growth and development of Richfield, Cameronton and Barkerville was steady after 1863. They gradually became mining towns rather than mining camps and soon contained the businesses, societies, schools and churches that relate to a growing society.

The Catholic Church was the first to send clerical representatives to Williams Creek. These came over at first from Antler to preach on a Sunday. Then in 1865 Father Gendre celebrated 11 o'clock mass every Sunday at Richfield. This did not long continue and he left, in fact, before the winter.

The following summer Father McGaggin arrived at Richfield, bought a house and prepared a place of worship.

By 1868 a Roman Catholic Church had been built. On July 19, Bishop L.J. De Herbomez, D.D., spent ten days at Richfield and dedicated the hall and bell of St. Patrick's Roman Catholic Church. Fathers Joliet and McGuicken preached the sermon.

The Church of England was represented by Reverend James Sheepshanks. In 1863 the sum of $1,200 was raised by contributions from the public, and a small church was built. Sheepshanks took into the church a library of two hundred and fifty books. None of the ministers or fathers remained long, and when Sheepshanks left, the mission became vacant for some years.

Reverend James Reynard arrived in Barkerville in the summer of 1868 and rented an old building which was also used for a school during the week. Here he held services every Sunday until it was wiped out by fire.

Reynard saw the necessity for a proper building for the Church of England in Barkerville and began to canvass for funds to build one.

The church was built in 1869, but the funds were very slow in coming in, and much of the interior fixtures had yet to be constructed. The priest himself helped with this work; and one piece in particular, a beautifully constructed little chair, built entirely without the use of nails, was attributed to him. The chair was completely put together with dowels. Finally, after many delays and setbacks, St. Saviour's Church was opened on September 18th, 1870. The church was standing on a mining claim and an application for free title to this land was made in April 1871.

Although this church had such a slow beginning it outlived all the others and stands today in Barkerville, with the appearance, particularly on the inside, of having been newly constructed.

To keep the church in repair, and to ensure that it would not be without a priest, it early became a custom, or unwritten rule, for the male parishioners to give a two-dollar offering at the services. This custom is still adhered to by the old-timers and by any others who know of it.

In addition to the Anglican and Roman Catholic churches, the Wesleyan Methodists were represented for a period of four months in 1863 by the Reverends Ephrian Evans and Arthur Browning. Then Reverend Thomas Derrick had a church built and dedicated in June 1869.

There was also a large gathering of Welsh people on the creek, and in 1866 John Evans was the leader of a group who eventually built the Cambrian Hall. Even though this was lost by fire, Evans had it rebuilt on the old site, but for various reasons this new one had no great success.

By far the most popular representative in the Cariboo before Confederation was the Presbyterian minister, Reverend D. Duff. He held morning services for the Church of Scotland at Cameronton and afternoon services at Richfield. He even remained throughout the winter months and stayed for a period of thirteen months in all, the longest that any clergyman remained on the creek at one time.

Various banking concerns were early represented on Williams Creek. One of the first was a private bank, that of A.D. Macdonald, who had founded his bank at Victoria some years before. He opened a branch at Barkerville in 1863, with a Mr. Crocker in charge. However, the main branch failed and the branch closed its doors within a year of opening.

The Bank of British Columbia, backed by British capital, opened at Richfield in 1863, moved to Cameronton and again to Barkerville, two years later. This was in charge of a Mr. Russel when it first invited business on the creek.

In addition, there was the Bank of British North America, which opened at Richfield in 1865 and moved to Barkerville the next year, with Robert Merril as manager. These last two banks remained on Williams Creek at Barkerville until 1872.

Many of the bank buildings were crude affairs, particularly in the first years. Walter Young, the manager of the Bank of British Columbia when it was situated at Cameronton, described it as a draughty two-room shack, with board walls lined with cotton and paper. The "vault" was merely a two-by-three-foot iron box, two-and-a-half feet high. It had but one lock and no combination.

By 1865 so much comment and publicity had been given the Cariboo mines in the papers in the south and even in Britain and Europe that a man by the name of George Wallace decided that what was needed was a paper published at the scene itself. About the 20th of May that year he arrived at Barkerville with a plant ready to go into printing. He had originally worked on newspapers in Victoria and was well qualified for his work.

The first issue of the *Cariboo Sentinel* was published June 6, 1865. In the months that followed, the paper contained interesting editorials, discussing various needs of the communities and the miners, many advertisements from businesses of the three towns, besides news other than local. A few of the many advertisements that appeared are quoted below:

HARDWARE
Building material, locks, butts, bolts, et cetera.

Carpenter and blacksmith tools.

Blasting powder and patent safety fuses.

Nails cut, and wrought iron and copper, all sizes.

Scythes, snathes, stoves.

Bar, sheet, hoop and band iron.

Gold scales 32 ounces & 64 ounces.

STATIONERY
Legal cap, note and foolscap, envelopes, ink, pens, blotting paper.

Weekly time books, violin strings, song books et cetera.

A. MacKenzie,
Barkerville, Williams Creek.

READING ROOM AND CIRCULATING LIBRARY
Cameronton, Williams Creek.

$2 per month. One hundred volumes of new works.

John Bowron, Librarian.

HENRY LAMON
Richfield

Commissioned Merchant, Liquors sold

Wholesale and Retail. Storage.

The best stabling of horses to be found on the creek.

Hay and oats always on hand.

THE BANK OF BRITISH COLUMBIA
Incorporated by Royal Charter

Capitalization $1,250,000

Branches and agents in Victoria, Yale, Nanaimo,

Mouth of Quesnel. In United States, San Francisco,

Portland, Oregon.

Current accounts opened for any amount. Bills

discounted. Gold Dust and Bars Purchased,

Received on deposit or advanced upon.

Cameronton, Williams Creek

LAGER BEER BREWERY
Barkerville

Chantceller & Nicole Prop.

Beer $4 gallon. Sold by quart, gallon or 2-1/2 gallons.

MOSES HAIR INVIGORATOR
W.D. Moses

Next door Madam Bendixon.

In the first issue of the paper a letter written by Dr. John Chipps is of interest:

Sir:

In the summer of 1863, there were typhoid symptoms which proved fatal to some. During the past season frost bites and scurvy have entirely vanished. Better cabins and a plentiful supply of vegetables have caused this. The cold, though intense, was unaccompanied by the piercing wind so frequent in other countries. During the winter months only three patients were admitted to the hospital. One had diseased lungs, another was a case of rheumatism and the third an accident. The general health of the creek is good and I've no doubt that a moderately warm season and plenty of "dust" will keep both body and mind healthy.

I am,
Yours obediently,
John Chipps, Physician at W.C. Hospital

The *Cariboo Sentinel* was destined to operate for a period of ten years. It was first a weekly, then a bi-weekly publication. In October 1865, George Wallace sold his interest to Allan Lambert, who had worked on the Victoria *Colonist*. He in turn, after a short period, sold his interest to Robert Holloway, who continued to publish until the paper closed its doors. (In the meantime Allan Lambert went south and began the well known *Yale Tribune*.)

Joshua Spencer Thompson, one of the five original members of the Hard-Up Company at Grouse Creek, was at one time an editor of the *Cariboo Sentinel*.

The mention of typhoid fever by Dr. Chipps is significant. Outbreaks of this disease had been frequent throughout the Cariboo, particularly among the Indigenous population farther west of Williams Creek. One of the members of the first group of miners on Williams Creek, William Cunningham, had only the year before died of typhoid, or "mountain fever" as it was frequently called by the miners. He died on June 21, 1864, at Soda Creek, then the terminal of the Cariboo Road.

By 1870 enough wives and children were on Williams Creek to cause the residents to rent a school. Then by public subscription and a small government grant a schoolhouse was built. By the first week of September 1870, Miss Clarkston from New Westminster arrived and opened the school doors. This school was so much needed and such a success that in 1871 the government set up a school district with a board of six. John Mundell was given the job of schoolteacher and with seven pupils he opened the first public school in the Cariboo. He remained, however, only to the end of March 1872, and for the next two years the school was closed.

In 1874 Mrs. Thompson reopened the school with sixteen pupils, and it continued in operation until 1905 when it was again closed for a short time. Some of the Barkerville children attended school at Quesnel during this time, some at Yale. However, it was not very long before they again went to school at Barkerville, excepting those in the higher grades.

Mail service in the Cariboo was in the early years a most uncertain thing. Often important letters or documents were delivered by private hand at great expense to the sender. As much as $5 for the delivery of one letter was not uncommon. But as soon as the trails to Williams Creek allowed the pony express companies to travel to the mining towns, much of the mail was carried by these companies.

As early as June 1858, W.J. (Billy) Ballou established the first express between Victoria and the Fraser River mines as far as Lytton and Kamloops (then called Fort Thompson). In September of the same year D.C. Fargo did the same between Yale and Lytton. At first Ballou's means of transport was one canoe.

F.J. Barnard was the first expressman to carry mail into the Cariboo. He began this service in November 1861, and incredibly he was able, by carrying the letters and papers on his back, to walk or snowshoe the distance from Yale to Cariboo and back. This was seven hundred and sixty miles return. One can only imagine what his hardships must have been. The next year he led a horse loaded with letters and parcels into Barkerville, thus establishing the first express service into the camp.

When the Cariboo Road was completed in the fall of 1865, allowing teams, wagons and stagecoaches to travel to Williams Creek, all services were greatly improved. The next year, 1866, a post office

One of the stagecoaches operating on the Cariboo Road. Courtesy A. McGillivary

was opened at the library building at Cameronton and John Bowron was appointed postmaster.

Prior to this time, there had been small post office services at Richfield or Barkerville, some years at one place, some at the other.

This service was supplied by the express companies. They and others had their own stamps to facilitate handling of the mail. Some of these stamps were quite elaborate and were in different shapes, with the names of the issuing express companies printed on them. The Wells Fargo's stamp was of a triangular shape with a base of nearly two inches. When the goods, parcels or letters were delivered and paid for, the stamps were affixed and marked paid; or, as the case might be, were affixed and marked paid at the time the mail was given to the companies for delivery. These stamps are rare collectors' items today.

The Chinese had a definite place in the social life of all the mining towns. Although at first the miners attempted to keep them out of the goldfields, it was not long before they were forced to hire them in the mining operations. It shortly followed that the Chinese settlers opened businesses. A large number, too, followed the rush, and as the

White settlers left a claim or an area, they took over, gleaning a better than average living out of their toil.

Quesnel Forks is an example of a place that became in time an almost entirely Chinese community. Here were joss houses and a Chinese Masonic Hall and other institutions. It was quite a large settlement, probably the largest in the Interior, and was a favourite wintering place for the many Chinese working throughout the Cariboo.

A sidelight on the Chinese miners in this area relates to the great Bullion Mine, located not far from Quesnel Forks. There the lead was first discovered in the latter part of the 1800s, when scores of Chinese miners were combing the area in search of gold. Who knows but that some of them were, even then, working on the very ground which was to produce such great amounts of gold in the years to come! The Bullion didn't come into prominence until the twentieth century when Mr. Hobson began its operation. In later years, Mr. and Mrs. Sharp owned and operated this mine, which had been the largest hydraulic operation on the North American continent.

Wherever there was mining there were Chinese miners. Many of the prominent merchants in the Cariboo today are the descendants of Chinese miners and businessmen who came with the gold rush, and remained, as did the White population, because the Cariboo was "in their blood."

Barkerville had its Chinatown right from the start, with its stores, hotels and other businesses. Their cemetery was above the canyon on Williams Creek.

The Chinese settlers followed their ancient sacred custom of sending the remains of departed ones back to China for burial, so that their spirits might seek celestial peace in their homeland. Every seven years, bodies were disinterred from the graves. It was not unusual to see two or three of the older men carefully cleaning the bones before packing them for the homeward journey.

Throughout the 1860s, the mining carried on, and new discoveries and improved methods of mining were continuously being made. During the mining season of 1865 the claims were not paying as richly as in former years, but nonetheless a far greater number of mining claims paid well and gave moderate and steady incomes to their owners. The output of gold was very little less than in the two years following discovery.

However, there had been continued dissatisfaction with the government on the part of the miners, and by 1866 the editor of the *Cariboo Sentinel* felt compelled to state his own feelings on this matter. In the summer of 1866 he wrote:

A little over two months have elapsed since the miners arrived, and already over one million dollars has been taken out in gold. There are now approximately two thousand miners in the district. If this territory were under a government that would foster and encourage the mining population instead of grinding men down by exceptional taxes so as to force them to leave the colony there would be four or five million dollars instead of one million in two months. It is well known that within a very few miles of Williams Creek there are innumerable gulches and creeks capable of sustaining an immense population and yielding easily $5 to $6 to the hand, but they are completely neglected and unworked, simply because miners will not stay where the government seeks to drag the last cent out of their hard-earned money for taxes to support its iniquitous extravagances. The population of the Cariboo this year is not a half of last year, yet there is an increase of nearly a half million dollars over the same period of last year.

Despite this dissatisfaction and these complaints and despite the decline in population, enthusiasm continued, and every year found new men coming in to prospect, mine or even to set up businesses.

Barkerville was now becoming the undoubted centre of the creek, and the men and women there felt it was time that the small town had a theatre of its own. A few of them gathered together to form the Cariboo Dramatic Society and in 1867 began to raise funds for the building of a theatre. The result was the Theatre Royal which was officially opened in May 1868.

John Bowron was one of the leading figures in the dramatic society, which remained active for many decades. The society put on plays, readings and had singing groups. Besides this, any outside entertainers now had a definite place in which to perform.

One of the original members of the society was James Anderson, a native of Perthshire, Scotland, who came to the Cariboo in 1863.

He put out a small book of verse which was first published by the *Cariboo Sentinel* in 1868 with a second edition in 1869. His book was composed of songs in which he had cleverly put new words into old country tunes. He wrote under the name of "Sawnee." The Songs of Sawnee early became a rare book and a collector's item.

Anderson had a beautiful singing voice, and it was in the capacity of a singer that he performed in the Dramatic Society's efforts.

The summer of 1868 was dry and warm. There was such a drought that some of the mining operations had to be suspended, and large fires were raging in the vicinity of Richfield. These fires continued on into September. But little did the people of Barkerville dream that their entire town would be destroyed by fire in this fateful month. The terrifying fire that wrought this havoc began in Barry and Adler's Saloon at two on the afternoon of September 16. There were various stories about its cause, one being that a miner knocked down a lamp in a friendly scuffle; and another, that one of the women ironing her clothes caused the blaze. But no blame was attached to any one person in particular then nor in the days that followed. Everything was tinder dry at the time, and the houses and buildings were so closely packed that flames leaped from one to another. Within an hour practically nothing was left but smoldering ruins.

Those closest to the fire when it first started could do little to save any of their goods, but those on the outer rim did manage to carry out some of their possessions. It was estimated that in all only about one-quarter of the contents of homes and businesses was saved. Looting began almost immediately, and when men came back to get their saved possessions, they found many items missing that were known to have been carried clear of the rapidly spreading fire.

At the upper end of town, Scott's Saloon was saved. It was adjacent to the Barker Company's ditch and flume, and the water from this was responsible for the men being able to prevent it from catching fire. At the lower end the raging flames abated somewhat and stopped just short of McInnes's Saloon, which was also saved. J. Weill and the Hudson's Bay Company had their warehouses below this and these two escaped destruction. The latter company, Hudson's Bay, long prominent in British Columbia, had opened a store at Quesnel in 1866 and one in Barkerville in 1867.

After the first wild frenzy, the people realized their helplessness and took the fire and its destruction almost calmly. They stood by quietly watching the town and their homes devoured by flame.

By nightfall hundreds of men, women and children were to be seen racing in every direction as they sought shelter for themselves and their goods. Women and children struggled with pots, pans, bedding and even beds, while the men carried great sacks of flour, beans and other produce. Goods and effects were scattered along the length of the creek and even on the hillsides. All must be stored, and a place of shelter found for the night. Surprisingly every man, woman and child found a shelter, some in deserted cabins far up on Conklin Gulch.

The next day the first appraisal of damages was learned. The greatest single loss was that suffered by Strouss's Store. This was estimated as being $100,000. The losses ranged from $1,500 up to this figure. Some were as follows: Hudson's Bay Company, $65,000; Lecuger & Brun Hotel, $20,000; Cohen & Huffman Store, $32,000; N. Cunio, Brewery, $40,000; B.N.A. Bank, $10,000; Masonic Lodge, $4,000; Kwong Lee Store, $40,000; F. Castagnetto Store, $33,000. The total loss was close to a million dollars.

The smoldering ruins had scarcely cooled when the people of Barkerville began to rebuild. A few decided to leave and forsake their businesses, but the majority remained. Less than a week after the fire, on September 22, twenty buildings had been erected, with the foundations of several others laid. A shortage of carpenters and tools was all that delayed the rest from beginning to build. Some of the twenty rebuilt establishments were Strouss, Mason & Daly, J.H. Todd, Bowron's post office, Dodero's Store, and Rebecca Gibbs' dwelling. Besides these twenty buildings, eight or ten Chinese houses had already been rebuilt.

Among the more than hundred homes and businesses lost in the fire were: J.C. Beedy's Store, Moses's Barbershop, Dr. Carrall's home and office and Madam Bendixon's Hotel. Besides these, there were such buildings as Barnard's Express, the Theatre Royal and the Bald-head Company's shaft house. Over three hundred people were made homeless.

Most of the buildings were completely rebuilt by 1869, the Theatre Royal among them. The Mason's Lodge was not completed until eighteen months later. (This lodge was again destroyed by fire in 1936, and still another one was put up in its place, which is in use today.)

A letter written by John Bowron to the Postmaster General on April 19, 1870, shows one of the side effects of this fire. At this date the post office was about to be moved from Cameronton to Barkerville and his building abandoned. Since John Bowron had put up the building at his own expense, spending well over $1,000, he wrote that he felt the government should pay him rent for the years he had operated, since he was left with the building on his hands and could not hope to dispose of it for even half its cost of construction. The amount he asked for was only $380, which was $20 a month since the fire. However, the government in answering his letter declined to agree. After passing his request from one to another person, the final answer, a copy of which was sent to him, read:

> The building in which the post office and library were before the fire belonged to the government. Mr. Bowron was Librarian and Postmaster when Barkerville burned down. Mr. Bowron built the post office and library on his own responsibility as he could not otherwise have obtained the salary of Postmaster. He expressed no intention of charging rent, nor was any promised, or provided for by the government. I don't think he is entitled to anything, more especially now that he is re-instated.

Discouraging as this undoubtedly was to John Bowron at the time, it was not to be for long. He was destined to play an important part in the affairs of Barkerville. Not too long after this—early in 1872—he was appointed mining recorder at the government office at Richfield; and from then on his progress in government was steady and sure.

The rebuilding of Barkerville seemed to please all who had lived there. They said the town was a better planned and a better-looking place than before.

In the next decade, the seventies, when hydraulic mining began, the tailings from Stouts Gulch, Walkers Gulch and even parts of Williams Creek began to accumulate on the lower section of the creek, and around the buildings and houses of the new Barkerville. In time it was to become necessary to raise the buildings and put in a log cribbing foundation. The sidewalks, too, were raised and supported on posts. This allowed all water and tailings to flow freely under the buildings without obstruction.

The Theatre Royal in the thirties.

There had always been a fire protection company on Williams Creek, known as the Barkerville Fire Company, but after the Great Fire, the Williams Creek Fire Brigade was formed. Headquarters were in a fire hall in part of the rebuilt Theatre Royal. The well-organized fire brigade was made up of twenty permanent members and many volunteers.

To serve the new brigade, water tanks were built on the hillside well above the town. From these, the water was piped down to hydrants, which were housed, together with hose and equipment, in cabins. One of these cabins to this day serves its original purpose in Barkerville.

Two of the original hose-reels, one of which is still in use, exist today in Barkerville. Several sections of the leather hose have been preserved.

A large number of leather pails which formed part of the original equipment have been stolen in recent years by souvenir hunters. The main advantage of leather pails was that, when a bucket brigade was formed which led to the roof of a building, the last man could throw the empty pails to the ground without damaging them.

Two bells, one on the church and the other on the old Theatre Royal, served as the fire alarm. The latter bell, now hung on the hose tower adjacent to the present day community hall, is still in use as a fire alarm in Barkerville. The other bell hangs in St. Saviour's Church; when it is rung at odd hours by visitors, residents of Barkerville still run to their doors in case it may be a fire alarm, although modern fire sirens have long since been installed in the community.

The Chinese citizens of the early community had their own subsidiary fire brigade, the equipment of which showed a great deal of practical ingenuity. A cleverly contrived and effective type of fire-pump, constructed of hollow bamboo and manually operated, could hurl streams of water from buckets on the ground onto flames on the roof-tops. Some of these remarkable pumps can be viewed by visitors today in Barkerville.

Barkerville of more modern times had a completely volunteer fire brigade of approximately eighteen members, including Fire Chief Bill Hong and deputies, as well as volunteers from the whole town if a fire occurred.

Since the Great Fire of 1868 no major fire has occurred, any incipient blaze being so effectively attacked by the Williams Creek Fire Brigade that it was brought under control before amounting to a conflagration.

The last dance at the Theatre Royal, 1938. Courtesy W.T. Ward

11
OCCUPATIONS NEW AND OLD

With the advent of hydraulic mining there came into being another industry for the tinsmiths of the area since much of the hydraulic pipe necessary to carry the water from ditch and penstock to the monitor was assembled at Barkerville.

The first tinsmith to assemble this pipe was John Bibby. In fact, for many years his shop was the only source of pipe. Previously he had built stoves and stovepipes. The material for these was brought in as flat sheets, which he cut and assembled. Many of the gold pans used by the miners were also made by him. But it was the production of hydraulic pipe that made his business a thriving one.

The iron for this pipe also came in flat sheets which he cut, rolled, crimped and riveted. There were many different sizes of pipe necessary, depending on the size of the plant being installed. Some were huge affairs, four feet in diameter, tapering down to three feet, in eighteen-foot lengths. Others were two feet in diameter and over several hundred feet of pipeline tapered down to nine inches.

Many sections of the pipe that John Bibby made are still used by placer miners in the Barkerville area. These are easily distinguishable by his method of setting the rivets in the pipe. It's interesting to note also that his first plant for assembling hydraulic pipe is still in the district. This consists of a set of rolls, much like a washing machine wringer, four feet in length. These are turned by intermeshing heavy bronze gears, manually operated. There are also the crimpers, rivet press and other interesting pieces of equipment belonging to the plant. The last tin shop he built still stands in Barkerville just behind its original site. A large, hewed-log building with sheet copper roof, it is in excellent condition.

Both John Bibby and his brother, James, were interested in the mines in the district and invested their money in a number of them. They were on the directorates of several mining companies, such as the Proserpine and the Waverly. On the latter board, they held their positions for many years.

James Bibby owned a large stable from which he rented out saddle horses, horse and buggy outfits and freight teams. His special pride was a team of handsome white horses, probably Percherons. On the rental of these he was most particular and would not rent to just anyone. In some cases, he chose to drive the team himself rather than leave it in charge of someone he doubted. James Bibby developed several hay meadows by cutting the trees, even ploughing and sowing timothy and red top hay. The "Bibby Meadows," of which several are still extant, are a familiar name in Barkerville.

Besides numerous quartz veins throughout the district which intrigued the miners from the beginning, great interest was taken in a stretch of meadowland below the town of Marysville. "The Meadows" extended for several miles along Williams Creek and continued beyond it where the Willow River flowed through them. There was considerable talk during the sixties of forming a company to take over the entire meadow area to explore it for gold. Any effort to work the ground had so far failed due to inability to cope with the water flow. The miners in the district were very much opposed to one company having complete control over such a large area, and even though no one individual or small company could hope to finance such exploration, nothing came of the proposed company until in 1870 the Kurtz and Lane Company obtained a lease on five miles of the Meadows.

Even though this company now had a steam pump as well as two nine-inch Cornish pumps, the water, in the end, beat all efforts to mine the ground. Kurtz and Lane sank a shaft one hundred and fifty feet deep, then tunnelled in to a further depth of ninety feet. Their drift was seventy-five feet in length. The cost of this operation was $60,000, and they were able to obtain but two and a half ounces of gold. When they realized that the channel was much deeper than they expected, they abandoned operations.

In 1911 and 1912 the Cariboo Goldfield Company with a type of elevator dredge brought up gravel from an interglacial pay-streak which existed about sixty feet below the surface. This averaged about a dollar a yard for a while, but in the end was abandoned as the buckets, bringing up the gravels, were unable to withstand the abrasion of the rocks. The development was excessively costly.

In the 1950s, when dredging on the Meadows was given several years' trial, much gold was taken out, but still the costs exceeded the gold yield. Nevertheless, the company officials felt that they were just about in a position to make a heartening profit when a calamitous accident sank their washing plant and they were forced to cease operations.

A year or two before this, when the company had been dredging up the Meadows, they completely excavated the old bedrock drainage tunnel of the sixties which extended to the upper end of Barkerville. When the company reached the elevator dredge of 1911, which had at that time cut and blocked the tunnel, their operations cleared out this blockage. Immediately there was a great rush of water funnelling out of the tunnel and completely draining the entire underground area of Barkerville. This torrent of water disclosed the framed timbers and derrick of the dredge, which stood for some time before it was dredged out. The operator of the dragline was fortunate enough to find his machine sitting on the posts and caps of the old timbers and in line with them. He was able to maneuver it out of danger as the sand and material was caving out from under the tracks of his machine. Otherwise, it would have dropped forty feet into the dredge pond with the cave-in.

The Meadows still remain unconquered by man, and to a great extent their gold content remains a mystery. There are those who feel that a fortune lies buried beneath them in narrow gutters similar to that of Williams Creek. Others wonder if the gold yield would ever pay for the operating costs.

The report that follows, written by John Bowron on December 4, 1896, to the Incorporated Exploration Co. of BC, Ltd., gives some idea of both the man himself and also of the general aspect of optimism towards the Meadows, which aspect is held by many to this day.

W. Thompson, Esq.;   Richfield,
Vancouver.   December 4, 1896

Dear Sir:
In response to your request for information obtained during my long term of office as Gold Commissioner of the Cariboo District, concerning the placer mining claims on Williams Creek with special reference to the ground lying below those claims, which have already been worked by drifting on bed-rock, I beg to submit, that during the very period when the gold output was at its greatest, that is prior to 1874, no official returns were made. Many of the claims that produced largely then are being profitably worked today.

It is roughly estimated that from twenty to twenty-five millions of dollars have been won from the working of the placers on Williams Creek and its tributaries, commencing at the lower line of the Cariboo Goldfields properties, and extending up-stream a distance of two and a half miles, the width of pay gravel varying from 50 to 200 feet wide. This large output from so small an area has probably not been equalled in any part of the world.

Below the Cariboo Goldfields' lower line, the bottom of the deep channel has never been reached, although several shafts, varying from 60 to 120 feet in depth, have been sunk. In all these shafts good prospects were obtained, but owing to the pumping plants not being of sufficient capacity to cope with the large amount of water encountered, the attempts to reach bedrock were abandoned.

This ground is regarded by old miners here as the most promising investment in this section to offer capitalists, who are prepared to undertake the work of thoroughly exploiting the ground. With this view I quite concur.

A hard stratum of clay or cemented gravel is found on Williams Creek above the rich stratum of pay dirt near bedrock.

This stratum is impervious to water, hence the diggings may be kept from the influx of the accumulated moisture of the surface.

After the deepest part of the channel has been definitely determined by means of the boring machine it becomes then a comparatively simple proposition to sink a shaft in bedrock at the side, and then drift out to the desired point in the channel.

The numerous small creeks and streams that flow into this portion of Williams Creek have all been worked more or less profitably. The existence, therefore, of gold in the main channel is almost beyond doubt.

From my personal knowledge I can confidently recommend the ground known as the "Meadows" on Williams Creek, to any company possessing sufficient capital to develop it.

In order to properly illustrate the information asked for, I have engaged Mr. Phelps to prepare a map of Williams Creek to be forwarded to you, and which I am sure you will find very useful.

I remain,
Your obedient servant,
(Signed) John Bowron
Gold Commissioner.

The year 1911 saw the mining of the Meadows with a hydraulic elevator dredge. But to this day the area has not been proven or disproven as a source of gold.

While the miners in the Cariboo were toiling on their claims, hundreds of other men were working at the task of bringing food, equipment and other necessities to the mining camps. The men who drove the mules and pony expresses over the first rough, perilous trails, and later brought the stagecoaches over the completed, but still crude Cariboo Road, led an adventurous life, both gruelling and dangerous. An entire book could be written about the express companies, freighters, pack trains, stagecoaches and cattle drives of the Cariboo Road.

The hundreds of men who through the years were engaged in these occupations faced raids, robberies, illness, exposure, broken equipment, and often the trials of miry trails and roads held them up for hours and days at a stretch. Many of them died of exposure and intense cold; others were wounded or killed in skirmishes. Still others broke down their health by packing into the camps before trails could even bring in mules. But for all that, a sort of glory surrounded these men. They were a breed apart. They took pride in getting through, in conquering obstacles, and braving weather conditions unfit for man or beast.

As mentioned earlier, F.J. Barnard was the first expressman to reach the Cariboo goldfields. He had travelled this great distance, seven hundred and sixty miles return, by foot or snow-shoe. Judge Howay, in writing of this feat, in Volume 2 of his *British Columbia* (published 1914), says, "the hardships and exposure endured by the expressmen in this hard winter of 1861, travelling over ice and snow, keeping open the lines of communication with the interior were perhaps never equalled in any country."

The next year Barnard led a horse loaded with express from Yale into Barkerville. His express service progressed steadily each year and in April 1864, he advertised his first stage coach service from Yale to Soda Creek, then the terminal of the Cariboo Road. With relays of horses every thirteen miles, this trip took only forty-eight hours and was a twice-weekly service. In the first year fifteen hundred passengers and $4,619,000 worth of treasure were carried.

It was during this first trip that Steve Tingley took some of the relay horses on ahead. On the return trip he took charge of the stage.

Freighting in the Cariboo. "Early days on the Cariboo Road"; driver William James Nelson with horse team and freight wagons ready to pull out. Image A-00504 Courtesy Royal BC Museum and Archives

To quote Judge Howay again: "(He) drove continuously from that time to 1897, during which time he rose steadily from driver to partner, to director, to manager, and at last became sole owner of the business, which was then known as the British Columbia Express."

Steve Tingley was known as one of the best stage drivers of the period, and early acquired the reputation of being the crack whip on the road. The title was in recognition of his speed in travelling the miles from Yale to Soda Creek.

This is but a brief outline of some of the first express and stage-coach companies. There were many others. Besides the stage operators there were the freighters. These worked at first largely with mule teams. In 1866 there were over two thousand of these animals owned by over seventy merchants and packers. Shortly, however, horses came to be used to a very great extent in this capacity.

Bill Livingstone, well known in the Barkerville area, for many years drove teams up the Cariboo Road between Ashcroft (south of Clinton) and Barkerville. His father had been one of the early packers on the trails leading to the Cariboo. Bill was born at Savona, BC, and was said to be the youngest freighter on the road. He later drove salesmen or "extras," as they were called, between Ashcroft and Barkerville.

In 1913 he settled at Quesnel as manager of the Inland Express Company. Even after the railway reached Quesnel, Bill continued freighting from that town to Barkerville.

Freighting team leaving Ashcroft. Second from right is "Soapy" Smith, of whom it was said that he would "Sooner fight than eat." Photo A. Mcgillivary

Before the teams took the express, stagecoaches and freighters up the road, there were the packers, who began almost immediately taking in supplies on foot. Later came the pack trains and the adventurous life of the men who handled them.

The following is a brief account of a day in the life of a packer and his horses. It began at dawn when he brought in a string of twenty to thirty horses to where the piles of supplies were ready to be packed.

These supplies included hundred-pound sacks of flour, sugar, potatoes and other fresh vegetables, case goods such as eggs, canned goods, hardware, cooking ware, pots and pans, even stoves and heaters, bed rolls and mattresses, tents and windows; all for a camp in the making, a mine or a store.

The packers first sorted out items of even weight to compose a balanced load for each horse. A hundred pounds of vegetables might be placed on each side of the horse with a case of eggs on top, giving an approximate two hundred and forty pounds balanced load to each horse. As nearly as possible each animal was chosen for the type of load he was most fitted to carry. Eggs were placed on a horse of a quiet nature, one that wouldn't get excited if he ran into trouble on the trail.

When all the supplies were packed and tied to each horse with the famous diamond hitch (which formed a diamond over the top of the pack and held it securely to the saddle), the horses would string out behind the lead mare. One of the men always took the lead to the trail.

Two or three of the horses had bells on them. These served several purposes. The steady tinkle of the bells let the packers know that all was well with the string. A rapid change in the tempo indicated trouble and one of the packers hurried to the distress signal, to adjust the cause. Even other horses in the string pricked up their ears at any change in the bells. They served a further purpose of warning wild animals of approaching danger, thus keeping them out of the way of the pack train. Seldom, if ever, did the train have problems with bear or moose.

To anyone who happened to be travelling with the pack train, it was a constant source of amazement to see how adept the animals were, and how quickly they became accustomed to their task of packing. How easily they inched around a large tree, twisting their bodies so that their pack would not bump or get caught! When going through a swampy bog or stream-crossing they stopped, then eased in with their front feet and slowly walked through. Never did they jump or flounder through if it could possibly be avoided.

As the morning progressed the packers were on the lookout for a suitable stopping place for a noon lunch, preferably a place where there was water and grazing for the horses. Allowing the animals a short time in which to rest, they ate the lunches which they had brought with them and soon were on their way again.

The packers were faced with many problems. The narrow trails often wound through tall timbers, up steep grades, then over slippery rock shale and down again into gullies that contained bogs or swiftly flowing streams. The men must keep the horses shod. Shoes could be pulled off by tree roots or be loosened or lost in rocky stream beds. A kit of shoeing tools was one of the necessities of the trail. Other problems were the saddle galls that sometimes became a cause of concern if a poorly adjusted pack had rubbed against the horse and created a sore. Such a horse might be laid up for several days, his pack divided among three or four other horses, while he followed along in the string.

On large pack trains, as on small, oats were packed on one or two of the horses for noon stops, if there was no grazing, and for overnight stops, when each horse got a half to a gallon of oats night and morning.

Camp equipment and supplies were packed on "camp" horses so that as soon as the overnight stopping place was reached, they could be taken off first and a meal prepared. This was sometimes in a trail cabin or just over an open fire. Meanwhile, the horses all stood where they were, waiting to be relieved of their loads. As soon as this was accomplished, the animals each acted in a different way. Some lay down on the ground and rolled about, others wandered away and started to graze, still others just stood about waiting for their oats.

It was a most comforting feeling to sit and relax in the pack-camp in the evening, men and beasts fed, another day on the trail over and night closing in.

When Antler, Williams, Grouse and Lightning Creeks became settled, transportation facilities were so remote that all the fresh meat was brought in on the hoof.

The first cattle drive recorded as having brought beef animals into British Columbia was part of the Palmer Expedition in 1858. The party consisted of thirty-six men and was bound from Portland, Oregon, for the Fraser River, over the inland route.

The records show that the next person to bring cattle into British Columbia was a trader by the name of Wolfe from Fort Colville, who came through with a herd not long afterwards. The cattle were brought up through the Okanagan Valley, and at one point some local Indigenous men raided the camp and stole about sixty head. These two herds are believed to have been the foundation of cattle ranching in the Okanagan and Fraser Valleys. Ranching was the first enterprise to follow the miners, and many ranches were taken up and settled. Some of these subsequently developed into the largest ranches in Canada.

To supply the winter market at the mines, there were generally two cattle drives in the fall, one in September and one in October, with between one hundred and one hundred and fifty head in each drive. Prior to 1863, the drives followed the Keithley-Antler-Richfield trail; later, they came through Quesnel, Cottonwood and Stanley, to Richfield. Many of these herds were brought in from the Okanagan and Nicola Valleys and from Clinton and the Fraser.

When the herds arrived, they were ranged on the alpine meadows of Bald Mountain or Mount Murray until freeze-up; then a few animals would be brought down each day for butchering and storing for the winter in sheds, and (in later years) in ice houses. Up until the 1930s, the slaughter houses were in evidence at Black Jack Creek and above the Bibby Meadows.

The strangest story, from today's standpoint, is of the hog or pig drive. It seems that in the early days, three to four men, generally Chinese, with several dogs would set out from Quesnel with seventy-five to a hundred pigs, and herd the uncooperative creatures up the trail to Richfield and Barkerville. The trip would take from six to eight days. Feed lots and camps would be established along the road.

Not many years ago, Joe Mason's son, Gordon, recalled how he had witnessed the beef drives as a boy. He said his father ranged his cattle on Mount Murray and also had kept a dairy ranch at Pleasant Valley. In 1963 the grandson of Joe Mason's buyer made a trip into the Cariboo and asked if someone could show him where the ranch was. The buildings of this ranch still stand at Pleasant Valley, about three miles out of Barkerville, a reminder of the early years of the gold rush and the varied occupations connected with gold mining.

Visualize four or five cowboys herding about one hundred to one hundred and fifty head of wild-eyed cattle up the narrow street of Barkerville.

"The beef drive is here!" The word passes quickly from house to house and up the street to the stores. As the drives come into Barkerville, from summer until late fall, there is great excitement. Dogs go wild and race around the fringe of the herd. Chickens squawk and cackle. Mothers wonder, "Where are the children?" Everyone comes out onto the verandah, porch or balcony to look over a sea of cattle. This is the fresh beef that will soon be served on the tables in the homes and hotels of Barkerville, and throughout the area for the next month or so, or until the next herd arrives. The odd tinkle of bells, a loud bellow here and there, a cow's moo or grunt in response to a sharp horn in the ribs, add to the excitement.

A merchant stands by the rail of the verandah of his store, note-book in hand. (It may be Joe Mason, or Daly, or in later years, A.S. Rogers.) He is waiting for his buyer to bring him the exact count of the cattle. These are his cattle, purchased by his buyer from ranchers and farmers in the Fraser Valley and the Clinton area. Some will be bought and taken to outlying camps at Grouse Creek, Cunningham Creek and Willow River. Others will be ranged on the mountain slopes until wanted.

How welcome is fresh beef, after the monotonous diet of canned fish, oysters, pickled herring or storage beef with that slight taint! In from the many surrounding creeks will come the miners and prospectors to enjoy their first meal of fresh roast beef in months. Invitations will be extended, and festivities will abound. The town is in a festive mood and all routine is interrupted.

The Chinese miners will be here too. They will buy beef according to the needs of their group; some leading one animal to their camp, others two or three. They will stake the animals out and feed them until more beef is needed. It is said that the Chinese are expert herdsmen, as they seem to temper the wildest animal in a few days. Soon the beast becomes content and feeds on local grass, getting a shine to his coat and fat on his ribs.

Such were the beef drives! Now and again the odd stray wandered off up the back street to be challenged by the local milk cows, or was found browsing in someone's garden. The beef drive was an occasion. It had been going on since 1862, and would continue until improved transportation made it unnecessary. Every year saw an improvement. In the early years it took weeks from Quesnel Forks, Keithley and Antler. Very shortly there was a trail from Quesnel and the drive was completed in days, with the stock in much better condition on arrival.

The last beef in the fall were grazed until freeze-up, when they were butchered and stored for winter use. This October drive brought the last fresh beef that would be seen in the town for many months, for not until May or early June would the welcome cry again run through the streets, "The beef drive is here!"

During one of these drives of the early years an unusual hold-up took place. Each merchant had his own buyer, to whom he gave bank drafts or cheques. The independent buyers always carried cash. In this particular instance, one independent, who was known by his white "gum" coat, had brought in his herd and made a successful sale. At the same time he also sold his raincoat. He and his hands stayed in Barkerville for a few days, as was the practice, to enjoy the life of the miners, so different from that on the range.

However, the man who had bought the gum coat left for Quesnel next morning. On the second day of his trip, as he rode down Mexican Hill, he was held up by gunmen who demanded his money—the money they expected him to have from the cattle sale. The robbers, after being convinced that this was not the buyer, and that all this man had on him was seventy-five cents, took the coat and the victim's horse, leaving him to walk. His first stop was Cottonwood House, where he told his story. The incident became known in the camps as the Gum Coat Hold-Up.

Johnny Boyd, whose father was the owner of Cottonwood House, quite vividly recalled this incident and the victim walking in and telling of his experience.

Almost as soon as the prospectors passed by on snowshoes, a little roadhouse would pop up to supply meals, overnight stops for the men, and later hay and stabling for the horses. Early in 1861 Red Davis established a store seven miles up Keithley Creek on the trail between Keithley and Antler.

The well-known Littler's cabin was established in this same year on a level grassy flat on the divide between Antler Creek and the Swift River. Littler, an ex-pugilist, was later Billy Barker's bodyguard at his mine during his prosperous years.

Other places on the trail between Keithley and Antler were Veith's Store on Little Snowshoe Creek and Porter's stopping place at old Antler Town. Porter's was the last place of this kind in the old town. Mrs. Kenvick was still operating the post office at Veith's store as late as 1940. Boyd's Cold-Stream House was established on Boyd's farm, in 1860, on the trail between Quesnel and Quesnel Forks.

When the trail was completed from Quesnel to Lightning Creek, and later from there to Richfield, many roadhouses came into being.

Boyd & Heath, owners of the Cold-Stream House, built Cottonwood House twenty-one miles out of Quesnel in 1864. Also farther down the Quesnel-to-Barkerville road on Pine Grove Creek was Edward's House. Lord Milton and Dr. Cheadle related that they had had a splendid meal there when they passed through in 1863. There was the Beaver Pass House as well as a roadhouse between the old Eagle Creek Bridge and Barkerville, which was operated by two Black men, who lived happily uninvolved in the big trouble down south.

The proprietor of Beaver Pass House, Mr. Peebles, was one who by nature radiated a home-coming welcome and extended to each person such attention that the guest came to feel he had been included in the family. The house was remembered by all who rested or dined there as a delightful experience in Cariboo life.

Approximately one and a half miles down the pass is the site of one of the first brick kilns of British Columbia, and many of the bricks made at this kiln are still to be seen today. It was found that the clay and sand for the making of bricks existed almost on the same site. The brickmakers were some of the many diversified tradesmen attracted to the area in search of gold. Installation of the boilers for the deep-lead mines made it necessary to have bricks made in the area. Mr. Pinchbeck was the brickmaker at the Beaver Pass site.

It was through Beaver Pass, too, that the first northern Railway Survey was made in 1889. The proposed line terminated at Bowron Lake and was to be known as the Great Eastern and Pacific Railway.

What tends to be forgotten about the period are the immense hardships suffered by these men as they packed into the new unmapped territory. For example, those men who arrived at Antler in mid-winter on snowshoes had to dig a resting place out of four or five feet of snow before they could bed down for the night. Here, with material cut from nearby trees, they built an A-frame, filled it in with more rough lagging, covered the whole with branches of trees, and then piled it completely over with snow. With a fire in front of this it afforded a warm shelter in below zero temperatures.

Even after the men had found pay dirt on the various streams, they were faced with the task of setting up their shaft houses in deep snow. They always cut enough lagging, posts, and material for the shaft collar, to get them down at least four feet with their shaft, before they started to dig. The ground is not frozen under this great depth of snow, but once this is lifted, they must work fast to get all done and covered before the exposed soft ground has time to freeze. When the shaft collar freezes, this is all to the good as it prevents cave-ins and water seepage.

The winter weather conditions of the Cariboo are pretty rough, but those on Williams Creek and surrounding areas are even more so. The men coming from the south and the coastal regions must have been at first unprepared to cope with a winter that began in October and lasted until about the middle of May. The skittish temperatures which might be twenty below one day and thawing the next, the snow that still lay in shaded areas in June, the occasional snowstorms and frequent fierce hailstorms of the summer must have appalled those who first lived through them. Barkerville, at an altitude of 4,200 feet, and Richfield, even higher, were the places where storms began. It is no wonder that very early in its discovery Williams Creek was referred to as a place where "there are nine months of winter and three months' poor sledding."

As the years progressed and the settlements of Antler, Carnarvon, Marysville, Cameronton, Grouse Town and at last even Richfield faded and passed into history, Barkerville persisted. It came to be the centre for all the prospecting and mining ventures of the region.

A small item from the Hudson's Bay Company's records, written October 9, 1882, aptly describes the decrease in population and business that had begun to be felt even earlier:

> As the yield of the gold mines on which this place depends entirely has been falling off, and the population diminishing in late years, we think it would be advisable to withdraw gradually, and when the present stock of goods there can be disposed of or greatly reduced, to close out...It has been necessary to keep a considerable stock of goods at Barkerville for we have always had a large share of the trade, and latterly nearly the whole of it...by the end of next year the goods and debts may, we hope, be realized so far as to admit of finally closing out...what may remain (including the buildings) can then be taken charge of by Mr. Skinner of Quesnel...the disposition of the buildings will probably be the most difficult thing, but possibly someone may be found to purchase or to lease bye and bye.

It happened that the buildings were taken over and a store business carried on continuously from that date until sometime in the late thirties. The premises passed into various ownerships beginning with a Mr. Wilson, then A.S. Rogers, Harper, Tom Nichol, J.F. Campbell and finally Mrs. L.M. McKinnon purchased it for use as a warehouse.

From a one-time total of over five thousand, the population of Williams Creek dwindled to two or three hundred, centred at Barkerville. This total often trebled during the hydraulic season when miners returned to their various claims.

On the hillsides of Williams Creek and its tributaries Stouts, Conklin and Mink Gulches, and on the Barkerville road itself are traces of what were once rough trails leading to the hundreds of cabins that were built there. Most cabins have long since been used for firewood by newer generations, but now and again their sites and some remnants of them can be found today. Some of them are still standing, surrounded by a hundred years of tree growth; in the mind's eye they bring back to full flood the tide of men who, by their purposeful activities, opened the vast resources of this far western Canadian province, then only a Colony of the Crown.

When much of the glory was gone, men and women who had settled in Barkerville remained, some surviving there even into the next century. These, perhaps unknowingly, perhaps in full awareness, kept alive the memory and the history of the gold rush on Williams Creek. Their occupations, old and new, very fortunately continued; otherwise too much would have been lost forever.

12
THREE GENERATIONS

There were men who came to Williams Creek who were destined to remain there for their lifetime, drawing from the adventurous days a fullness of life until then unknown and since unequalled. Five of these that come readily to mind are I.B. Nason, Andrew Kelly, John Houser, John Bowron and Charlie House. These men in particular did, of themselves and through their descendants, contribute greatly to the life on the creek from their arrival and on into the next centuries.

The first of these, Ithiel Blake Nason, was one of the comparatively few men in excellent financial circumstances when he arrived at Antler in 1861.

Of Scottish parentage, he was born in the state of Maine. He had travelled to California when still a boy and was there in time to take part successfully in the 1849 gold rush. He was a slim, lanky man with an easy manner and confident nature.

At Antler his ample funds allowed him freedom to take time to prospect extensively. Here he put down two or three shafts a short distance from one of Antler's tributaries, Wolfe Creek, and was successful enough in one of them to drift for a distance of a hundred feet, taking out some gold.

He was one of the early miners on Williams Creek. He and his associate W.A. Meacham held the Deadwood and Forward Claims. The former claim, at the mouth of Mink Gulch, whose waters flow into Williams Creek, was not very rich, but the Forward for some seasons could hold its own with the other rich claims on the Creek.

By 1863 Antler was beginning to wane and there was not the necessity for a sawmill there as in the first few years. Meacham and Nason therefore decided to purchase this mill and have it moved to Williams Creek. This they subsequently did. The plant, the first on Williams Creek, did not use the circular saws of today. Rather there were several straight saws mounted on a shaft. The shaft turned, powered by a water wheel, accomplishing the working of the gang saws. This method, known as drag sawing, was a great improvement over the whip saws in general use at the time.

The sawmill came into immediate use and operated successfully at Richfield for many years. Lumber was in constant demand on the creek and it eased the work of the miners considerably to be able to get it "at home" rather than to manufacture it themselves or have it packed over from Antler.

By 1866 the partners had done so well that they decided to invest in a more modern sawmill. They finally chose and purchased a steam sawmill from Quesnel that had been built by G.B. Wright and Jerome Harper for the intended purpose of cutting lumber for the building of the Steamship *Enterprise.*

In August 1866, Nason and Meacham bought this mill and transported it to Mink Gulch, about a mile above Richfield, and near their claim, the Deadwood. Their advertisement in the August 27th issue of the *Cariboo Sentinel* most fittingly describes this new sawmill:

> WILLIAMS CREEK SAWMILL COMPANY
>
> The undersigned lumber merchants beg to inform the inhabitants in general of Williams Creek that they have now in operation a Steam Saw Mill located at the mouth of Mink Gulch above Richfield, capable of manufacturing 1000 feet of lumber per hour, any length, any width required in the market, and of a Superior Quality. All orders left with Mr. W.A. Meacham at Barkerville, or the mill, will be promptly attended to and delivered Free of Charge at any point on the wagon road and at Reduced Rates. The undersigned trust to merit a liberal share of the public patronage and that their old friends will kindly give them a call.
>
> MEACHAM, COOMBS & NASON

In 1879 I.B. Nason, ever keenly interested in mining, was one of the six original shareholders in the Waverly Hydraulic Mining Company and one of its trustees. He played an active role in the company for many years. Besides this, all the lumber for the operation of the mine was supplied to the company from his mill, and it continued thus for years.

It was shortly before this that he married Mary Watson, the daughter of Adam Watson, who had emigrated from Scotland to San Francisco in 1850. A large family was born to them at Richfield and there the children spent their early years.

Nason led a busy life in the ten years following, taking an active part on the boards of different mining companies and continuing the operation of his sawmill. He erected still another one at Jack of Clubs Lake, as well as occasionally conducting some mining on his two claims on Williams Creek.

Then in 1889 Nason became a member of the Fifth Legislature of British Columbia's history, succeeding Robert McLeese. He had by this time moved his family down to Barkerville and while parliament was in session they remained there. Meanwhile he returned to Williams Creek whenever his duties did not keep him at Victoria.

It was during his fourth year at Victoria, while parliament was in session, that Nason died, in 1893. His widow moved away at that time from the Cariboo and with her children went to live in Victoria. Oliver Nason, one of the younger sons, returned to Barkerville in 1904 with his uncle Bill Watson. He was sixteen at the time and spent his first summer working on the tramways at the Hard-Up Claim at Grouse Creek.

He and an older brother, Blake, remained in the Cariboo with their uncle until the outbreak of the Great War, when both enlisted. It was from these years with their uncle that the brothers gained great knowledge of the life at Barkerville and Richfield. Bill Watson and his friends had countless tales of the mining days which gave the brothers much insight into life on the creek in gold rush days. Oliver Nason had a keen memory, and those accounts he had gathered when still a young man in his teens remained with him the rest of his life. He knew so much of the where, why and who of the early claims and also had such a store of anecdotes both witty and interesting, that in later years he dreamed of someday producing a book, feeling certain that the appeal of these stories would guarantee its success. The war years spent in the trenches in France seriously undermined his health; and it was some years after the war before he came back to Barkerville, returning with his wife, Lillian, in 1932. One of the first things they received in the mail was a tax notice on the Deadwood and Forward Claims which, being real estate claims, were kept up just by paying taxes. Presumably someone else up to that date had paid the taxes, and this was the first time that Oliver had known that the claims were still in good standing. The taxes on these two claims have been kept up since then to the present time.

For many years Oliver and his brother Blake interested themselves in the mining industry. One of their developments was on Antler Creek below Beggs Gulch. Here they sank a shaft in the hope of drifting out a gutter which was known to be gold bearing. Their results were only marginal, returns being about four ounces to the set.

An accident took the life of one of the men who were partners with them. They had had great difficulty in controlling the water and slum, and this necessitated the use of false sets and face boards. As they continued drifting upstream the pressure of slum increased. This finally resulted in the face caving in. The slum and water burst forth with such pressure that it carried the two men on shift through the tunnel and up the shaft. Only one man escaped injury. He was floated to the top of the shaft and was able to crawl out. The other was caught up among the timbers and was drowned. The collar of this shaft and the remains of the water wheel can still be seen at the "Nason" shaft.

Another of their ventures was with the Houser brothers. Blake Nason had gone to school with these boys, and they had many joint projects. This one was on Canadian Creek and is called the Houser Shaft. It was not a success and again water was the powerful enemy. For the first time in this area, they used steam power to run their pump and hoist. The Houser brothers' undimmed conviction that gold existed in paying quantities on Canadian Creek led them to sink many shafts there, the last in 1946 and 1947.

After many years of prospecting in the Barkerville area, Oliver did considerable work for local mining companies. His last was as hydraulic foreman for the Lowhee Company. In the summer of 1955, he left to go to the Shaughnessy Hospital in Vancouver, and since he was to be there for a lengthy stay, the Nasons decided to leave the Cariboo. When Oliver was released from hospital, they made their home at Vernon. On March 1, 1959, he passed away, leaving his widow and only daughter, Verna.

When one considers his incredible memory, and the fact that he knew many of the old-timers who had arrived in the sixties and seventies and heard from them and from his uncle so many little-known facts concerning the history of Williams Creek, practically from its beginning, one realizes the immensity of his loss to Barkerville.

Andrew Kelly, a young man of Irish parentage, came to Antler in the fall of 1862 from Victoria. Later that same fall he travelled over to Richfield and proceeded to below the canyon with the intention of securing a claim if possible. However, he was by trade a baker, and as he looked about him at the hundreds of miners and prospectors who had arrived with him and saw other men putting up business buildings, he decided to do the same. From his own experience he knew the great need of the miners for fresh bread and baked goods.

By the next year, 1863, he was the owner of a claim and, adjacent to it, a bakeshop. On the shop was the sign: Wake-Up-Jake Bakeshop, Coffee Saloon, and Lunch House. By 1864 his claim, the Wake-Up-Jake, had reached bedrock and found a rich paystreak. For the next two years both the mine and the bakeshop were highly successful. The claim, however, was not one of the immensely rich ones, and most of the gold was taken out in the first years.

With the discovery of the Heron claim on Grouse Creek there was created a tremendous rush on that creek, and many of the miners and prospectors from Barkerville and from other camps in the district left or sold their holdings and proceeded there, among them Andrew Kelly.

In March of 1866 Kelly married Genevieve Lipsett-Skinner at Victoria. They remained in Victoria for some weeks, then travelled to Williams Creek. Early in May, Andrew sold an interest in his holdings at Barkerville to a man named Patterson. Very shortly after this, having decided to locate at Grouse Creek, he sold the remaining interest to a Mr. Goodson. As soon as possible he and his bride proceeded to Grouse Creek. Here he built a substantial boarding house and added to it a large bakeshop.

His bake oven was the commonly used brick oven of that day, but generous in size. This can be one of the simplest forms of ovens known and can be built by anyone anywhere using nothing but clay and rocks. First, a floor is laid with flagstones and then the sides and top are formed with rocks and clay in such a way as to form an oval. The back of the oven is built up to form a chimney, and the door is fashioned of a large piece of tin or flat rock and made to fit tightly into the oven. The whole oven is completely encased in firm earth; in fact, the very early ovens were built around a hole dug into the earth.

Andrew Kelly's oven was much more elaborate than this and was built to contain dozens of loaves of bread, pies, cakes or cookies at a time. To bake the bread a fire was lighted in the oven and the door closed. When the bricks were sufficiently hot, the ashes were raked out, the bread put in and the chimney blocked.

The boarding house was built on a mining claim Kelly had staked below and adjoining the famous Texas claim. Although this claim was never as rich as the Texas, he continued to work it until it was mined out.

The boarding house was opened on Sunday, July 22, 1866. Remnants of the building itself and of the large bake oven are still visible on Grouse Creek.

Thus it was that young Mrs. Kelly's first home in the Cariboo was on Grouse Creek. Here two of their children were born—in this new bustling mining camp where two small centres, Grouse Town and Boone Sawmill, were rapidly building up. They remained here for the next four years, then in 1870 decided to return to Barkerville. It was with considerable anticipation that they and their young family, having completed all business arrangements, set out by horse and wagon with such of their goods as had not already gone ahead of them.

Once arrived at Barkerville Kelly set about acquiring a building in which he intended to establish a new business. This was the Kelly Hotel which he opened in 1871. (He later purchased the adjoining building.) The sign which he hung out was a large octagon-shaped lantern, on the glass sides of which was printed, "Kelly Saloon and Beds."

At this same time, he purchased a large lot across the street from a man whose property had been lost in the Great Fire. The lower portion of this second lot was shortly sold to BC & Yukon Telegraph, who the following year put up an office building which also housed the government post office.

Some years later Andrew Kelly set the rest of the lot aside as a public playground for the children of the town. In the winter this was used as a skating rink. During the summer months it remained a clear, grassy spot in the busy street, and such it was until the 1930s, when a one-room schoolhouse was built on part of it.

The Kelly Hotel flourished and created for Andrew Kelly and his family a rewarding life in the steadily developing town. Here he brought up his family who, as they grew older, took their places in the community.

Sorrow, too, came to the Kellys. Their little boy, Johnny Hastie, born at Grouse Creek in 1869, died in his sixth year in 1875 and was buried in the Barkerville cemetery. Another baby died only two days after his birth in 1878.

Andrew Kelly kept his zestful interest in the mining of the district and had shares in mines on Grouse Creek, Proserpine Mountain and in the Hurdy claim at the upper end of Williams Creek. He, along with William Rennie, Joseph Mason, John Bibby and Ithiel Blake Nason, were the first directors of the Waverly Hydraulic Mining Company, formed in 1879 at Grouse Creek. He remained a director of this company until 1909.

In 1905 when he and his wife left Barkerville for the winter he bought a home at Victoria, and some years later they moved there permanently. They celebrated their golden anniversary at Oak Bay, Victoria, on March 16th, 1916.

When they left for Victoria in 1905, the Kellys made arrangements to have the piano, which had been carried from Quesnel to Barkerville in 1863, shipped down, with a view to having it repaired and tuned. This piano had survived the Great Fire, the owners at the time being some distance from where the fire started. Andrew Kelly said at that time that he had purchased the piano from Miss Nathan, who used to play it with her feet, and it had as a result lost some of its keys! With a twinkle in his eye he remarked that she had been quite hard on it. He continued, "After it is repaired and tuned, I'll return it to Barkerville for my grandchildren." The old piano was in the Kelly family for years.

One of Andrew Kelly's sons, William H. Kelly, made his home in Barkerville and followed his father's manner of life. After the senior Kelly left for Victoria, sometime in 1909 or 1910 William took over the managing of the hotel and succeeded his father as shareholder and as a director of the Waverly Hydraulic Mining Company. He had met and fallen in love with Lottie Brown, the granddaughter of a hotel owner at Richfield. She was a slim, pretty woman with dark hair and brown eyes, with a quietness of nature which in later years resolved itself into an inner radiance, which showed through in all she did. The pioneering spirit was in her, and like all pioneers, no task daunted her. No matter how impossible it might seem, there was

Ithiel Blake Nason. Photo taken at San Francisco in 1857.

nothing in her make-up to even suggest that it could fail.

She and William Kelly were married on September 1, 1901. By this marriage there were four sons, Walter, Russel, Bill and George.

The Kellys had been married for only sixteen years when William Kelly died in 1917, leaving his widow to bring up four growing boys.

Later Mrs. Kelly married Malcolm McKinnon, who had been in the Cariboo for many years. He was a jovial, open-hearted man with a marvellous sense of humour. He was an experienced man in placer mining operations and had held positions in a number of companies. He shortly became hydraulic foreman of the Lowhee Mining Company, which position he held until 1934. Three daughters were born to the McKinnons, Mabel, Christina (Teeny) and Mary.

As the Kelly boys grew up, they took over a good deal of the operating of the business. Russel had never been well, and he passed away in the thirties. Each one had his own particular part of the work. Walter handled the machinery end of things, the bulldozing and the keeping of all equipment in good condition, as well as the trucking. Bill Kelly drove the transport trucks and George managed the store. In later years the daughters took over some of the store and hotel work.

Those years were busy and happy when Malcolm McKinnon was working at one of the placer operations, first the Waverly and later the Lowhee, and when the hotel, store and transport trucks were doing a thriving business. Mr. McKinnon is remembered as the perfect host of his hotel.

He died in 1943 of a heart attack which he suffered while hurrying to help put out a fire. After his death Mrs. McKinnon, who had developed good business competence, took over the reins of the business once more, handling it for the second time alone. She made a forthright success of all their business ventures.

Mr. & Mrs. Andrew Kelly, pictured on the occasion of their golden wedding anniversary in 1916. Image I-60761 courtesy of the Royal BC Museum and Archives

The Kellys and McKinnons seemed to be almost a dynasty in themselves, with Mrs. McKinnon the typical matriarch. Their business was the last to operate in Barkerville—the last of scores of hotels, stores, cafes and freighters. The Kelly Hotel, which Andrew Kelly had opened with such enthusiasm in 1871, was in continuous operation until December 31, 1952, when it closed its doors after eighty-one years of service. This had not been an ordinary licensed house, but held its original charter, by which it had been in the early days permitted to sell liquors of all types.

Many reasons might be given as to the cause of the success of these remarkable people. The first thing that comes to mind is that they were conscientious and hard working. There was nothing slipshod in anything they did. An example of this was in the store. An item was never known to be forgotten in any order. Also, all orders were packed with a view to how they were to be carried. All one needed to say was "I'm packing this myself," and the items were packed in such a manner as to easily fit on a packboard. Similarly, orders for boat travel or by pack horse were specially assembled. There was never an error in the orders nor in the bill.

Credit was extended to any customer who was making an honest effort, and this was not just for a week or so but for a month or even months. A fellow who had had the misfortune of failing to clean up by fall, after a hard, gruelling summer, would arrive at the hotel knowing that his winter's room and board was there for him. There were no questions asked. In fact, it was taken for granted, someone

The Kelly Hotel. The water flume for domestic use and also the bell of the Theatre Royal are seen here. W. T. Ward. Image D-03919 courtesy of the Royal BC Museum and Archives

remarking, "Well, so and so is in for the winter. I guess he'll take the room next to Jim." His credit at the store took care of any personal necessities.

What was true of Kellys' Hotel and store with regard to credit was equally true of other businesses at Barkerville—the Lee Chong Store, Campbell's Hotel and Store, and before Campbell's, Nichol's. Knowing that one could get backing at these businesses was one of the factors that gave to the residents a sense of security. Many a man finding himself stranded far from Barkerville knew that if he could but get back he could obtain credit to make a fresh start.

The Kellys' equipment, their large cats, bulldozers and wood trucks, did a tremendous amount of work throughout the entire Barkerville area. Here again, there was no question of putting in time; all their work was accomplished with an efficiency seldom seen today, and with a view to completing as much work as possible in as little time as possible.

As for the freight trucks, one could set one's clock by the sound of Bill Kelly's truck leaving Barkerville every morning at five a.m. sharp. Bill was known to have been unable only once to get to Quesnel on the roads, which many times seemed impassable. On one other occasion he turned back at Stanley, but this was because the snow was so heavy it simply was not practical to proceed. As he pointed out at the time, "I could have made it all right, but it wasn't worth the time it would have taken."

They were and are a remarkable family. It is doubtful if such service as theirs will ever again be seen anywhere. It was faultless.

To them and to Mrs. McKinnon particularly, many people came with their problems, a serious one of finances or just the necessity of getting a wreath and proper burial for some man who had died alone and far from his family. Mrs. McKinnon grubstaked quite a number of the prospectors and even advanced the money for the purchase of homes for a number of families.

This family, starting with Andrew Kelly and Mrs. McKinnon's own parents, had more to do with the Richfield–Barkerville area, its economy and social life than any other family living and, for years after others had gone, was to remain the foundation of the town.

Mrs. McKinnon's two brothers, Alfred and Herbert Brown, who lived in the Barkerville and Stanley area throughout most of their lives, were like her in the thoroughness with which they did their work. They were responsible for a great deal of exploration work in the many gold-bearing creeks and streams in the area. Both were expert Keystone-drillers, and it was in this capacity that much of their work was done, not only locally but in many areas of the province.

Mingled with this sketch of the Kelly and McKinnon families in Barkerville are a hundred warm memories of the many people they knew or had close association with through the years.

Not the least among these people was their Chinese cook, friend and helper, Foo Fang Song, affectionately known to Barkervillites as Dear Song. Andrew Kelly was still operating the hotel when Dear Song first became a member of its staff back in the early 1900s. Some of Andrew's grandchildren were mere infants. They grew up with Dear Song always in the background, cooking the delicious meals, pastries and cakes which they, along with the guests, ate with such pleasure. He was more than cook. He was part of the family, old-fashioned, respectful and courteous, with an innate dignity he never lost.

Dear Song held an important part in the life of the Chinese people of Barkerville. He was highly respected and looked up to and was, in fact, one of the elders who in their tradition have kept the Chinese in a cohesive group with its own rules of etiquette and behaviour. He had come originally with the miners sometime during the late eighties and had retained his keen interest in mining. He assisted in the financing

Foo Fang "Dear" Song, the cook at McKinnon Hotel, Barkerville, 1916-1948. Courtesy Barkerville Archives

of his Chinese friends in their mining ventures, in many parts of the district, and no doubt received his share of any profit. Dear Song was missed by everyone in Barkerville when he passed away in the forties, after more than forty years of service in the Kelly Hotel.

Andrew Kelly's second daughter, Jeanie Kelly, married a man who was himself a Cariboo pioneer—James Alexander (Sandy) Locke. The Locke family was probably as well known throughout the whole of the Cariboo as any of the old-timers. Sandy Locke drove the stage between Quesnel and Barkerville for over seventeen years. He resided at Barkerville for a few years when he first took over the stage. Here he met and married Jeanie Kelly.

The Lockes lived at Quesnel for many years, until at the turn of the century around 1901 or '02, Sandy took over the old 13-Mile House on the Barkerville Road. He operated this until sometime in 1912 when he moved his family back to Quesnel so that the children might attend school. His daughter, Bess, married George Butterfield, who was one of the last stage drivers from Fort George to Quesnel. At that time the road followed the present Blackwater Road on the west side of the Fraser River during the fall and winter months.

At one time George Butterfield drove stage from Hixon to Prince George. Mrs. Butterfield recounts how the stage started out in November 1922, on wheels, but when the snow came they transferred to bob sleighs, as the roads were not ploughed out in those days. They stayed in Prince George that winter and she adds: "I was on the first launch to come down in the spring in May 1923. [Launches were

Kelly's bar, as it was in the last century.

used during the spring break-up.] The canyon was rough then, too. There were two passengers besides the two children, me and a box of chickens on board, as well as the mail and express. Jimmy Williams, now deceased, was the captain. We had a good trip down."

Mrs. Butterfield, before she was married, at one time worked at the Royal Cariboo Hospital at Barkerville and recalls many stories she heard of the old-timers. When asked why the hospital was moved from Marysville she said that one of the reasons was the difficulty in maintaining the bridge crossing Williams Creek which was fast becoming buried in tailings.

Laura Locke was married to Bill Livingstone, who as has been mentioned, was one of the youngest freighters on the road. Bill Livingstone was an excellent horseman and continued as teamster for the mines at Wells even after the trucks had taken over the hauling of freight from Quesnel. He was a well read and respected man. It is regrettable that the knowledge he possessed of the early days in the Cariboo has been allowed to pass unrecorded.

John Houser, of Irish parentage, was born in an eastern city of the United States but was brought up at San Francisco. He and all his

Henry Nicholas Brown (left) and Mary Catherine Brown (right) were owners of the Brown Hotel and early pioneers at Richfield. Photos taken about 1870.

family were musicians and played in the symphony orchestras of that city. He was an accomplished violinist, and it was a great boon to the miners when he came to Williams Creek in 1862 that he brought his violin with him. He had a good repertoire of selections and, as he had in San Francisco, he even wrote his own when the fancy for something different caught him. One or two pieces of his composition are still preserved by his granddaughter.

The San Juan Claim at the far upper end of Williams Creek was staked by Houser, and he began mining there by shaft and tunnel in 1863. For some years he took out good pay but, as this became depleted, he looked about for other mining interests and eventually was associated with several claims on the creek.

His was one of the names on the petition of July 1863 asking the government for an amendment to the *Mining Act*. He remained on Williams Creek for some years, occasionally returning to San Francisco for the winter months. It was on one of these trips that he married a Miss Suhs of that city on October 23, 1870. Their first son, William, was born in San Francisco the next year.

The following year John Houser brought his wife and young son to Williams Creek. They remained there for a year and then all went back to San Francisco. They felt at the time that they would not return to the rough life of the mining towns. However, as has happened to many, the Cariboo had claimed them for its own, and in the fall of 1875 Mr. and Mrs. Houser with their small family took passage from San Francisco on a coast steamer bound for Victoria on their way to the Cariboo.

This time Williams Creek remained their lifetime home. They settled below the canyon near Stouts Gulch. John Houser continued with his mining at the San Juan and at other claims. They both took part in the social activities of the town and soon became valued members of the Dramatic Society. Together they added much to any social gathering. It was the custom for John Houser to play the violin for any dances and parties on the creek. Later, when the children of Barkerville were growing up, he gave them music lessons. His own sons received their violin lessons from him and became very proficient, Johnny in particular. Two of the Houser boys, Johnny and Billy, followed in their father's footsteps, taking a keen interest in mining, both on his claim and on many of their own.

As a young lad Johnny Houser was one of the herdsmen for the dairy cattle that ranged on Cow Mountain above Stouts Gulch. He started during one of his summer holidays from school and continued for some years. On the top of the mountain were the corrals, stables and herdsmen's quarters. Here the cows were milked morning and evening. The milk was then put into specially designed cans which permitted them to be loaded on pack horses for delivery to the various settlements on Williams Creek. It was the herdsmen's job to milk the cows and once a day to deliver the milk. Johnny, speaking of this in later years, said, "When we arrived at the houses with the milk, the customers came to the door with either a tin pail or a pitcher, and we dipped the milk from our cans and poured it into their containers. By the time we completed our rounds the dipper had a liberal coating of cream. All this had to be washed up. It was quite a job cleaning all the cans and dippers when we got back to our cabins on the hill."

For many years, saddle horses were the mode of transportation in the district, and many people travelled for miles on horseback. Johnny said that it was nothing for a person to travel to Stanley or Quesnel and back on horseback, or to Antler and Keithley.

Johnny was an accomplished horseman. It was a pleasure to see the young, red-headed youth handling expertly a wily animal as he set off for some far mining camp or town. He married Belinda McCarthy, who was as interested as he in music. The two gathered a few of the young folk around them and formed a small orchestra with which for quite a number of years they toured the Cariboo, playing at the many dances in the district during the winter months.

John Houser's granddaughter Hazel, now Mrs. Walter Kelly, says she can vividly recall those days when her father and mother travelled with the orchestra. In those days babysitters were unknown and the family went with the parents wherever they found themselves in the Cariboo. Dances started at eight o'clock and lasted till morning. It was an accepted custom that a room was set aside for the children. The younger ones and babies were bundled up and went to sleep at the commencing of the dance. The older children might be allowed up for a little while, but soon they too slept in the room provided. The women took turns at checking to see that the children were safe and happy. Mrs. Kelly says that at the time she was a little one, perhaps two or three years old, and she can vividly remember the excitement and fun that the tour created.

The whole attitude at the dances was one of pleasure and participation. At midnight there was a pause for supper. This was not just a lunch of sandwiches and coffee but a sumptuous meal. The men, after the floor was cleared of dancers, brought in long benches and trestle tables, upon which the women placed steaming plates of food which they had prepared in advance and kept hot on a stove. All sat down and enjoyed a hearty repast. Then while the orchestra was tuning up for the next dance, the women cleared the tables of dishes, the men took away the benches, and someone "slicked" up the dance floor. Soon a tantalizing strain of music announced the resumption of the dance. Though feet might ache the next day, the dances were a source of wholesome fun for all.

The Houser orchestra might play for dances at Stanley, then go on from there to Quesnel, Alexandria, Williams Lake, 100 Mile House and even at times as far as Clinton on their tours. Often the stagecoaches had a placard with the name of the orchestra on it, announcing the dates the tour would arrive at the various places and when and where the dances were to be held. They were extremely popular, and their arrival was a much looked forward to event.

The Houser boys, long before this orchestra had been formed, worked on their father's claim, the San Juan. In fact, it was here that a dreadful accident occurred when Billy Houser lost his leg in a cave-in, at the age of nineteen years. He carried on through his life on an artificial limb. His determination to find a rich pay streak persisted, and he continued to mine until his death in the 1950s.

The father, John Houser, had died in the spring of 1900, but the sons continued to explore numerous little creeks near Antler, Grouse, Canadian (close to Grouse Creek), Williams and others. Happily, one of the mines rewarded them with success—the Ketch Mine, a few miles west of Barkerville.

Mrs. Houser, Sr., outlived her husband by many years. Her married daughters were anxious for her to come to live with one of them and to leave the Cariboo, but she was not inclined to do so and lived at Barkerville until her death on November 30, 1933.

Johnny Houser's two sons lived at Barkerville throughout their lives, and his granddaughter Hazel married Andrew Kelly's grandson Walter, and resided at Barkerville until the early 1960s.

Charlie House is another of the early miners whose name is alive today in Barkerville. He arrived at Williams Creek in the late 1860s, and for many years worked at his claim on Conklin Gulch, whose gushing little stream flows into Williams Creek from its eastern slopes below the canyon. He later had a claim at Jack of Clubs Creek, which flows into the lake of the same name about seven miles from Barkerville.

Charlie House was spoken of as one of the handsomest and wittiest men on Williams Creek. He was a tremendously popular young man, well liked and highly respected by all the miners of the district.

When Mr. and Mrs. Houser and their family arrived at Williams Creek in 1875, they brought with them Mrs. Houser's younger sister, Margaret, little thinking that she, too, was destined to become a permanent resident. Very shortly after their arrival, Charlie House fell in love with this pretty younger sister and her charming sense of humour. The next summer in July 1876, they were married, and a gay and blithesome wedding reception followed the marriage ceremony. Miners from all the creeks, near and far, attended. For many years afterwards any happenings on the creek were referred to as having occurred either before or after Charlie House was married.

The material for Mrs. House's wedding dress, which was of heavy blue silk, was purchased in San Francisco. In keeping with the lovely styles of those days it had a basque waist adorned with two rows of silk covered buttons and a full sweeping skirt, with rows of pleatings and flounces. The sleeves were trimmed with buttons and lace cuffs. Even though the "wasp" waist was a tiny twenty-three inches, there were in all twenty-four yards of material in the dress, which at $3 a yard brought the cost of the material alone to nearly $75. Mrs. House kept this wedding dress all her life, and more than fifty years later it was in beautiful condition with nothing to mar its original beauty.

The House Hotel, which was still operating during the 1930s, was established at Barkerville by Charlie House in 1885. This very soon became and remained a favourite stopping place for the miners on the Creek. Charlie House's great vitality and warm personality and Mrs. House's ability to make people feel at home and to surround the hotel with a homelike atmosphere ensured its success. Mrs. House kept a most wonderful collection of house plants in the hotel, which she tended with loving care for over fifty years.

One of these plants was the "Bob Heath" geranium which had been kept blooming since 1896. This was a rare and unusual geranium developed by Bob Heath, the original owner (along with Boyd) of the Cold-Stream House out of Quesnel. The flower has a single bloom, very large, with a white centre and petals shading to deep rose pink. Mrs. House got a slip of the geranium from Bob, who kept a garden on the steep slopes of Williams Creek. She and others were successful in developing healthy plants from slips. Her grandchildren and the Tregillus's still have them in bloom.

Four children were born to the Houses, and with the exception of one son, Joseph, they all lived out their lives in Barkerville. The two daughters, later Mrs. Tregillus and Mrs. McArthur, like their mother, had the pleasure of a sister's company through all the years of their life in Barkerville. The son, Joe, lived there until an illness in the 1950s forced him to retire to the coast. From 1934 until his retirement he was the hydraulic manager of the Lowhee Mining Company. The House's eldest son, Charles Wesley, died in 1917.

Mrs. House, as had her sister, outlived her husband who died in 1913, and for many years carried on the management of the House Hotel. She died in 1939.

The descendants of Charlie House, the McArthur and Tregillus sons and daughters, lived at Barkerville until the 1960s.

John Bowron was born in Huntingdon, Quebec, in March 1837. He was a tall, well-built, dignified young man with brown hair, blue eyes and a well-groomed moustache. He was educated at Huntingdon Academy and later studied law in Cleveland, Ohio. He had an alert, eager mind and a radiant personality, always dignified at all times in both action and words.

He was a member of one of the overland parties that made the heartbreaking trip across Canada from Quebec and Ontario to British Columbia. Starting from the eastern provinces, these parties went through the United States by steamship and rail to St. Paul, and from there to the Red River Settlement. The only mode of travel the rest of the way from Fort Gary to the Upper Fraser River was by foot. Once arrived at the Fraser they descended the river on rafts through the treacherous, swift-flowing waters, narrow canyons and dangerous rapids to Quesnel. Many of the men lost their lives on this last part of the journey. Those who were successful arrived at their destination in September 1862.

John Bowron was one of the many who chose to spend his first winter in British Columbia at the coast. He arrived at Williams Creek in the spring of 1863 and showed at once a keen interest in all about him.

In those first few weeks, he tramped the whole of the creek from the topmost claim at Richfield to the lower ones at Cameronton, observing the method by which the mines were worked, talking with the miners and in the evenings holding lengthy and inspiring conversations with men who were to become his lifelong friends. He found in them a readiness to exchange ideas and a desire in most to make life on Williams Creek as nearly like the outside world as possible. It was during those early weeks, and later, when he did some prospecting on his own, that he conceived the idea of forming a society where men could meet and talk and once again feel themselves to be part of the world of music, books and the arts that had been left behind on entering the goldfields.

In the summer of 1863 with a small group, he formed the Cariboo Literary Society. The first meetings were held in his own cabin at Cameronton. The next year money was raised by public subscription to create a library. The government supplied the building at Cameronton, and Bowron became the librarian. The library when opened contained three hundred volumes of standard and contemporary literature.

In this same year, John Bowron, searching for a means to add to his income, undertook to clean the black sand from the miners' gold. Often at the end of a gruelling shift at the mine, a man found himself with several pails and pans of heavy iron concentrates, gold and black sand mixed together. From this the gold had to be separated. It was a time-consuming, painstaking work and the miners were only too glad to have someone whom they could trust pan it down for them, for a small percentage of the gold.

When Bowron was appointed postmaster at Cameronton in 1866 it was just at the height of the excitement on Grouse Creek. In the inevitable rush that followed he found himself caught up in the excitement and for the first time felt in a position to take part. Gold mining on Williams Creek had been limited to a great extent to those who had substantial capital to invest. It was with a feeling of adventure and anticipation that he joined MacAlindon, Thompson, Shephard and Robertson in forming the Hard-Up Company on Grouse Creek in the spring of 1867.

Although in the very first season the gold output of the new company was $120,000, which encouraged them greatly, the pay streak was not a continuous one. Other seasons found much of the profit dissipated in underground exploration. Nonetheless they continued to work and drift for some years. Then finally they did just the necessary assessment work to keep the claims in good standing, until in 1874 they had them surveyed by O.G. Travaillot and the next year they were Crown granted. Though John Bowron did not take an active interest in the Hard-Up Company, it remained for many years a great pleasure to him to take a trip up to Grouse Creek and look over the mining operations.

Nearly a year after the great Barkerville fire, Bowron married Emily Edwards at Richfield on August 16, 1869. Soon thereafter he built their home at Barkerville. Four children were born to them, two sons, William and Eddy and two daughters, Alice and Lottie. This house was to remain their home throughout the years. In front of the house Mr. Bowron planted a row of cottonwood trees, one of which is still growing on the Barkerville street.

In 1872 he was appointed mining recorder, and three years later, in 1875, government agent at Richfield. Then in 1883 he became gold commissioner, a post he held until 1906.

Of the many things John Bowron accomplished and letters he wrote while holding these offices the one perhaps of the most value is a map he compiled in 1894 showing the early claims on Williams Creek and their approximate total yield in gold. Up until 1874 no official record was kept of the amount of gold taken out of the Cariboo. Any gold that had been declared for tax purposes was recorded. This would include gold sold to the banks, merchants or gold buyers.

This map is a valuable reference source today as it gives the names and position of over a hundred of the original claims on Williams Creek, with the estimated production of each claim. All this might well have been lost to history. John Bowron pointed out at the time that the figures arrived at were only approximate but represented the best opinion and information available. The total output of a few of the mines was as follows: Rankin, $75,000; Cameron, $800,000; Forest Rose, $480,000; Wattie, $300,000; Wake-Up-Jake, $175,000; Michaels, $50,000; Ericcson, $500,000; Barker, $600,000; Black Jack and Burns Tunnel, $675,000; Cunningham, $250,000; Abbott, $150,000; Steele, $600,000; Dutch Bill, $200,000; Forward, $100,000; and British Queen, $680,000. These figures represented gross recovery totals, out of which mining costs had to be paid, and the net then divided among the partners. Some of the mines were still operating profitably at that date, John Bowron stated, though the largest amounts had been taken out in the sixties.

At a later date, on September 13, 1898, at the request of the government, Bowron forwarded an estimate of the gold output in the Barkerville and Lightning Creek areas. His letter written to J.G. Mathers on that date reads as follows:

Dear Sir:

Yours of the 5th instant duly to hand asking me to give you an estimate of the gold product of the various creeks in the vicinity. This is very difficult to do as at the time the greater amounts were produced in the early sixties no account for the gold produced was kept. The first mining reports were in 1874, but roughly speaking the approximate total yield of the various creeks up to this time will be as follows:

Williams Creek	$23,000,000
Lightning Creek	12,000,000
Stouts Gulch	3,000,000
Conklin Gulch	2,000,000
Watson Creek	1,000,000
Burns Creek	2,000,000
Antler Creek	2,000,000
Mosquito Creek	2,000,000
Sundry small creeks and gulches—say	5,000,000

This is as I say speaking roughly but I think it fairly close.

You will I presume be over this way before you go below. If so you can see my reports (annual) from which you can judge as to how I arrive at the above figures.

Through all the years of his office as Gold Commissioner and his consequent familiarity with the dozens of different creeks, gulches and quartz ledges of the area, Bowron remained enthusiastic as to the possibilities of new gold discoveries. He was confident of the eventual development of the known quartz veins into successful mines. His faith in the Meadows is clearly outlined in his letter to the Incorporated Exploration Co. of BC in 1896.

In 1895 his first wife, Emily, died and two years later he married Elizabeth Watson of Richfield, Mrs. I.B. Nason's sister. One daughter, Aileen, was born of this marriage.

In 1904 he increased his interest in the Hard-Up Claim to one third, and he, Joe Wendle and Beech LaSalle, who had obtained the other two-thirds interest, undertook further development of this claim. They retimbered the drift and extended it beyond the original shaft; put down a new shaft and started drifting from there.

In the summer of 1905, they were about to give up when to everyone's pleasure they struck pay dirt. It is stated that the gold they took out gave them $70,000 each. Joe Wendle and B. LaSalle had both been working at the development and had enough money to contribute toward the cost of operating. But John Bowron had to pay for his share of the costs from his gold, which resulted in his net profit being less. Nonetheless there was sufficient to free him of financial worry, perhaps for the first time since arriving on Williams Creek in 1863.

In 1906 he retired from office and he and his wife left for Victoria where he bought a home with the intention of retiring there. But, sad to relate, he died in September of the same year.

John Bowron had given to Williams Creek forty years of service as postmaster, government agent and Gold Commissioner. Besides this he had started the first library in the community, the Literary Society and, along with his associates, the Dramatic Society.

Of his children Lottie Bowron was the one who continued her father's keen interest, optimism and faith in the Cariboo. Miss Bowron spent her schooldays at Yale, coming home for the holidays at Christmas and in the summer. When she grew up, she was for some years a teacher's counsellor, visiting all the little schools in remote areas where she encouraged the young teachers and helped them with any problems. Later she became the private secretary of Premier McBride in Victoria, a post she held for many years. During the First World War she was in the Beaver Club at London, England, where she met hundreds of the Canadian servicemen and was able to talk to them of home and give to many a homesick serviceman new hope and confidence.

Miss Bowron remembered many details of their life in Barkerville. She recalled that when a little girl her first chore was to water

John Bowron (left), Government Agent, and Herb Brown.

Fred Tregillus, centre, and friends at Bowron Lake. Courtesy F. Becker

the cottonwood saplings her father had planted. She took great pride in this task and each evening went the rounds with a pail of water for the small trees. She recalled, too, that when Richfield in later years was on the wane, many thought the government office should be transferred to Barkerville. "Father used to snowshoe up to Richfield in the mornings to open the office," she said, "and how we wished they would move it." It was a joyful day for them all when finally, at the turn of the century, the office at Richfield was officially closed, and John Bowron was installed in the old Nason house at Barkerville which had been rented for the purpose.

Although Miss Bowron did not spend much of her adult life at Barkerville she visited it at every opportunity, and up until her death in the spring of 1964, she returned for the two summer months every year for over twenty years.

Miss Bowron's recollections of early Barkerville days were many. She used to stand on the back porch of her home when a small girl and watch, with interest, the huge water wheel that turned and creaked as it revolved, pumping water from the shaft of what she believed to be the Wake-Up-Jake mine. She said the men would get down into the sluice box as they were cleaning up at night and speak in almost inaudible murmurs, and she used to wonder why. As she grew up she learned that this was the climax of the day's labour—cleaning up the gold from the sluice boxes—a serious and suspenseful business!

Of her father, when he finally retired in 1906, Miss Bowron said: "He was most restless, and seemed to be pining away as if homesick for his accustomed round of activities and associates. He sometimes visited me two or three times a day, where I worked in the government office, and seemed lost and insecure in his new environment."

13
THE ENDURING PIONEERS

There were, of course, many who came to the Cariboo and remained, contributing greatly not only to the life there, but to the continuance of optimism, effort and accomplishment of the towns. It is impossible to speak of all of these people of pioneer spirit but several others must be mentioned in any account of the period.

THE TREGILLUS FAMILY

Fred J. Tregillus was born at Plymouth, Devonshire on October 31, 1862. When a young man in his late teens he left England for Western Canada. His first work in Canada was for the Canadian Pacific Railway, then engaged in pushing the rails across Canada. He remained with the company long enough to attend the historic ceremony at Craigellachie on the morning of November 7, 1885, when Donald A. Smith drove the last spike, and the nation-building transcontinental railway became an accomplished fact.

During his years on the railway, he became increasingly enthused by the many stories he heard of gold in the Cariboo, and he decided that he would himself go there to seek fortune in a country that still seemed to be veritably a vast treasure house. He obtained his first miner's licence at Vernon from the man for whom the town was named, Forbes Vernon.

In September 1886 he arrived at Barkerville but did not then take up residence there, remaining but a short time. Although well past its heyday, the town was still a bustling centre, with six saloons, three hotels, many flourishing businesses and several hundred inhabitants.

For the next few years Fred Tregillus worked and prospected in the Van Winkle and Lightning Creek area. About eight miles below Stanley and some miles from the Beaver Pass House there is a Tregillus Creek, named after him for the work he did on this small stream.

In 1895 he, Harry Jones and a man named Price began an extensive program of mining at Lightning Creek. Their leasehold was composed of the old South Wales, Spruce and Point Claims. It was here in 1897 that they struck rich pay on a bench ten feet above the old worked-out channel, and all three men came out with small fortunes in gold.

A few years later Fred set out on a world tour, leaving Vancouver on January 1, 1900, thus starting the new year and the new century in a fitting manner. On this trip he visited many foreign lands around the world. His ship was in China during the Boxer Uprising, and he recalled that it was boarded by hostile Chinese inspectors who searched for someone whom they thought the foreign ship was harboring.

After over a year of travel, Tregillus returned to the Cariboo, this time settling in a small cabin not far from the Reduction Works about two miles out of Barkerville. This cabin remained his headquarters for the next few years.

In 1901, along with Harry Jones and Sam Montgomery, he again began exploring the Van Winkle and Point Claims, only farther down from their first strike. Here they sank a shaft from a level of five feet above the creek at the base of a steep hill, along which the old Stanley-to-Richfield Road was cut in 1885. The shaft was continued to a depth of forty-one feet where they again found a pay-streak nearly fifteen feet higher than the deep-worked channel. After continuing through the big boulders of this pay-streak for some twenty feet they struck bedrock. Here they found rich coarse gold, with some nuggets ranging in size from one half to six ounces in weight. They were able to maintain an output of from six to nine ounces to the set for some time, and this gradually improved until one set gave them fifty, and another seventy ounces in gold, though these were considerably above the average.

Not long after this success at Lightning Creek, Fred Tregillus returned to his cabin at Barkerville. He had fallen in love with one of Charlie House's daughters, and in April 1905 they married. Their three children were born at Barkerville. These were a son, Alfred, and two daughters, Margaret and Mildred.

The Tregillus family made their home in a lovely cottage on the street, just above the Williams Creek bridge. The two-storey cottage, with its porch, lawn and plots of flowers, retains even today an English air about it.

For many years Fred Tregillus worked in partnership with Tommy Blair, who along with his brother was the proprietor of the Blair Store at Barkerville. One of their developments was on the old Black Jack Claim, opposite Stouts Gulch. After considerable work they reached pay-dirt, about which years later Mr. Tregillus in describing the claim said: "The gold in the gravels was like fruit in a plum pudding."

In 1916 he, along with Tommy Blair and Pat Carey, acquired an interest in quartz (lode) claims on Proserpine Mountain held by Elmer Armstrong, who had done a great deal of work on these and had been exploring the area for many years. These claims did not come to fruition until the 1930s, when they were sold to the New Proserpine Mining Company. But in the meantime the four men did a tremendous amount of exploration work here, over a long period of years.

By 1923 Fred Tregillus and his brother-in-law, Joe House, together with F.W. Reid, were the joint owners of the Tree-House Claim on Cunningham Creek. For many years they carried on hydraulic mining in this area. Here the family spent a part of the summer vacation at a lovely site where their cabins were built, protected by cottonwood and other trees, with the creek just across the road, flowing calmly at this spot through the tranquil valley.

His son, Alfred, did not follow the mining so enthusiastically as had his father. However, he was the youngest dredge-master of his day, operating the Kafue dredge, when W.C. Moore was in charge of dredge operations at Whiskey Flats, on Antler Creek. At that time Alf was only nineteen years of age.

Fred Tregillus's interest in mining remained with him through all his long years at Barkerville, but he was keenly interested in many topics. He was a bearded, slightly built, slim man of less than average height, wiry and alert. His mind was keen, his memory amazing, and he lost none of these qualities but remained alert and interested even in his nineties.

Both he and his family were active members of St. Saviour's Church, where the girls' and Alf's voices, singing the old hymns, sent music ringing through the building. Following church service on a Sunday night it was common for a group to foregather around the organ in the Tregillus home for hymn singing and pleasant talk.

Each year the family took its holidays out of Barkerville. They travelled to different parts of Canada for a month of pleasure, shopping and visiting old friends. Tregillus and his two brothers, one from Nelson, the other from Calgary, occasionally got together for a reunion on these trips.

During one of these holidays, in 1947, Mrs. Tregillus suddenly became seriously ill at Kamloops, just at the beginning of their trip and died shortly thereafter. Mr. Tregillus became ill as a result of the shock and suffered from the weakening effect of shingles, which stayed with him for several years. Fortunately, however, he rallied and spent many more pleasant years at home with his family, devoted as ever to his beloved Barkerville.

Fred Tregillus died in August 1962, just two months before his one hundredth birthday. He had spent seventy-six years in the Barkerville area and was a direct link with the gold camp's great days as he had arrived at a time when many of the first pioneers were still there. He lived with the old-timers, saw many new discoveries made in the district, and was himself responsible for some of them. He will always be remembered as a man who exemplified the best in dedication to gold mining and, living a good life in the success he deserved, was always willing to open his home to visitors.

Joe Wendle

Joe Wendle first came to British Columbia when he was a young man employed by the C.P.R. in its exploration for coal deposits on Vancouver Island, the Queen Charlotte Islands and the Cariboo. While in the Cariboo near the Bowron Lake area he fell under its spell and decided in 1895 to remain at Barkerville. At that time, he was a well-built, broad-shouldered, good-looking young man in his early twenties.

In the years following he explored many of the creeks and gulches in the area as a foreman for one of the mining companies or in connection with property in which he had acquired an interest. There was scarcely an area in the eastern part of the Cariboo in which he did not work and prospect.

One of his earliest projects was in the Guyet, the claims of which were acquired in 1899 by the Cariboo Consolidated Mining Company. For the next few years this company under his management prospected and explored the grounds. Though not a great deal of gold was recovered Wendle was sufficiently interested to buy the claims from the company, and he continued for some time exploring the area, until in 1910 he sold his interest.

For several years he concentrated his attention on Cunningham Creek, where he and his partners mined a fairly satisfactory amount of gold by hydraulicking. However, the cost of operation for equipment and development work eventually exceeded the output, and though he and Beech La Salle continued off and on in the hope of finding a deeper and rich channel, they were unsuccessful.

One of the many mines and mining prospects at which Wendle worked and explored was the La Fontaine, where he was in charge of drilling operations at Anderson Creek. One of his most successful developments was that of the Hard-Up at Grouse Creek, with Beech La Salle and John Bowron. Many years later Mr. Wendle gave a vivid description of the eventual success of this operation.

After spending some months in repairing the water wheel, rebuilding the flume and re-timbering and extending the drift beyond the old shaft, they began to sink a new shaft. Drifting upstream for a distance of one hundred and eighty feet their tunnel still had not found the channel or the pay. As a consequence, at a meeting at Barkerville the three partners decided that one more week should be the extent of their endeavors, and that if they didn't find pay then, they would shut down, at least for the present.

In the last day's work of the final week, the men on the surface sent down a set of timbers, which unwittingly brought the mine to success. After digging in the mud sill ready to set up the posts and cap, the timbers were found to be eight inches too long. Rather than return the posts to the surface to be shortened, they decided to lower the mud sill. It was while they were so engaged that Joe Wendle happened to come down the shaft.

He at once noticed a change in the formation and asked the boys to give him a pan of this new, rusty looking gravel. This he took to the collar of the shaft and panned it out. Eight dollars' worth of gold lay in the pan. At once he had a carload of the gravels sent to the surface for washing. To their great amazement and delight they cleaned up sixteen ounces of nugget gold. Joe later related that there were some nuggets recovered up to the size of his thumb. *For some time they had been drifting just over the top of their pay!*

He took the gold with him down to Barkerville and after setting it in a pie plate on a small table in the front room, he went to the back to have a shave. Presently he heard a knock at the door, and knowing it would be John Bowron, he called to him to come in. How many times had John Bowron stepped in to ask the state of the mining operations at this claim, in which he had held an interest since 1867! How many little flurries of excitement there had been! How many false hopes!

"How did it go today, Joe," he called out, "not much change I guess?"

"No, it's going much the same," teased Joe. He knew that his friend could not escape seeing the plate of gold on the table.

Almost at once he heard the exclamation, "Joe, you've struck the pay!"

At this Joe came out, one half of his face still covered with lather, and explained to John just how this had come about.

After a short, excited conversation John Bowron asked if he might take the plate of gold to show his friends, and immediately departed, bearing the precious stuff with him.

Joe said that he returned some hours later with the gold intact. Obviously celebrating with his friends, he was in high good humour.

THE WENDLES

Both Joe Wendle and his wife, Elizabeth, were great lovers of the outdoor life and everything pertaining to it. They spent much of their energy in preserving various forms of wildlife, and in extending existing beauty spots in the district. During their early years in the Barkerville area both lost no opportunity to explore the many magnificent mountains and beautiful lakes and rivers in the district.

One of their favourite places was what was then called Bear Lake, later named Bowron, a large blue water lake about fourteen miles northwest of Barkerville. The winding wooded road that takes one to the lake passes a mountainous region where huge avalanches have torn great gaps of rock and large trees from the mountain slopes of what is fittingly called Slide Mountain. Finally the road reaches Antler Creek and about a mile farther on, having ascended a long, winding hill, it arrives unexpectedly at the summit, with a view of the water. From its beach one can see that the lake extends on and on around many an outjutting piece of land, and far beyond it are the great snow-capped mountains. A little farther along the shore, the Bowron River flows out of the lake.

On the hill overlooking the lake, the Wendles built a home in which they could glory in the breathtaking view of the blue lake as

Frank Kibbee—the first game warden at Bowron Lake Reserve. Courtesy F. Becker

they had first seen it. This was in the summer of 1915. The interior of their cabin was finished that winter of 1915 and 1916.

Mrs. Wendle was a competent artist who had studied in the East and here at the lake she found scope for her talent. She painted many pictures of local scenes and also, to gain skill, made copies of famous paintings. Some years later the home was completely destroyed by fire and she lost her paintings and paint materials. They rebuilt the house on the same site, but unfortunately, she did not resume her painting after her disheartening loss.

The lake became the Wendles' home and life, and in 1926 they built a guest lodge on its shores. It was a two-storey log building with a wide verandah on two sides, from which one could view the boating and swimming and other natural attractions and beauties of the lake. Within was a large stone fireplace in a generous-sized living room. Joe Wendle did much of the indoor finishing himself; he also constructed some of the rustic chairs, tables and even the bedsteads.

Beginning at Bowron Lake, there is a chain of lakes over which one can travel by boat and portage for a distance of a hundred miles in a circle tour to Indian Point Lake and then by foot for the last twelve miles back to Bowron. Frank Kibbee, who had a trapline on the lake, and who built the first house there in 1907, had taken Mr. and Mrs. Wendle on this tour and they were so impressed with its many splendours that Joe was possessed of the idea of preserving all the wildlife within the waters of these lakes in a great game reserve. He spoke to a number of people of this idea and attempted to interest the government in investigating its possibilities, at first with little success.

In relating how he finally managed to accomplish his aim, Mr.

Wendle said that one summer they happened to have the provincial game warden as a guest. Joe said to him, "I could take you on a trip that you'd never forget." It was then arranged between them to make the journey around the lakes. The game warden was every bit as impressed as Joe had confidently expected. When they returned home, Joe then outlined his entire plan of not only creating a beautiful game reserve, but also making it possible for tourists and photographers to enjoy the trip. He wanted to have a narrow-gauge railway over the portages and a car to transport the boats from one lake to another.

Joe Wendle—his last hunting trip, 1949. Courtesy F. Becker

Shortly after this, the game warden prepared a written thesis expounding Joe Wendle's ideas and presented it to the legislature. It was as a result of this that the Bowron Lake Game Reserve was officially established in 1925. The narrow-gauge railway was used by hundreds of people, local residents of the area and grateful tourists. Frank Kibbee was appointed the first game warden of the reserve.

Another place of interest to the Wendles was only four miles out of Barkerville. A short distance off the Bowron Lake Road are two small lakes, surrounded by a park-like growth of trees. Because of its proximity to Barkerville, and also because the lakes were reasonably shallow for some distance from their banks, they envisioned it as a natural playground and swimming spot. Joe Wendle had this declared a park area and then set about having the foreground cleared of any undergrowth. He built two dressing houses of rough logs and also a small wharf and raft from which any who wished could dive into the water. It soon became a favourite picnic spot, and was named Wendle Park, enclosing Wendle Lake.

The Wendles encouraged the wildflowers already growing and also planted others. Besides this, fish were introduced to the lake and allowed to multiply. Not many years later it was possible to go to the little lake to do a spot of fishing. Their interest in wildlife never abated, and for many years Mr. and Mrs. Wendle officially banded birds for Washington DC's Migratory Birds of North America. They banded not only geese and ducks, but also many smaller birds. They have often related an instance of having banded a small bird which—if the name is correctly recalled—was a Fern Hawk. Forty-eight hours later this bird was shot and killed, literally thousands of miles away in one of the central states!

In his over seventy years of life in the Barkerville area, Joe Wendle contributed much to the district, and until shortly before his death, remained keenly interested in every phase of the development of Barkerville and the surrounding area. In 1958 he was presented with a Certificate of Merit by the Lieutenant-Governor and the premier of British Columbia for his contribution to the development and prosperity of the Barkerville community.

In the Wendle home are many souvenirs of the early days and of their very full and thoroughly enjoyed life. They have one of the original Hudson's Bay Company freight canoes, which Joe had obtained for their excursions on the lakes. He purchased this from Quesnel and had it brought to Bowron Lake.

Mrs. Wendle, besides being an accomplished artist, was also an excellent horsewoman. She and Joe travelled by horseback over the numerous trails that abound in the Cariboo.

It was on one of these trips when they were out hunting on Slide Mountain that she accomplished the amazing feat of killing two grizzly bears within minutes. Joe was not right at hand when, as she was travelling along, she suddenly saw a grizzly bear rise up from "nowhere." She wasted no time in shooting it down. Then before she had time to collect her thoughts, she saw what she took to be the same bear rise up again and fired another shot. As Joe came along, she said, "I've shot a bear."

What was their amazement when they went over to the spot where she had fired to discover not one but two grizzly bears lying where she had shot them!

In later years when discussing this feat Mrs. Wendle said, "I would certainly never want to have to do a thing like that again."

Joe had the hides cured and they kept them on the wall of their hallway, where for years they were the subject of excited comment by all who learned of the story.

Mrs. Wendle has often commented on how very much she and Joe enjoyed their life together at Bowron Lake and of how glorious were those days when the outdoors was their home, and the many trails, mountains, rivers and streams were theirs to explore and enjoy to the fullest.

William Brown

William Brown came to the Cariboo by way of Antler in the early 1870s. He was a man of prodigious strength, renowned for his many feats of endurance. He worked on countless drifts and shafts throughout the area from Antler Creek to Jack of Clubs Creek. For many years he resided in a cabin and prospected on the latter creek where he ran extensive drifts, some of them as much as four hundred feet in length.

He was a most independent man and revelled in his ability to outwork any man. It is said that the few times that he worked for other than himself he would not stay if anyone in the crew could accomplish more than he.

An example of one of his feats of strength exists in the cabin he built for himself. This cabin was at least twelve by fourteen feet in dimension, and was constructed of heavy logs, none less than eighteen inches in diameter. These Brown cut, peeled and skidded to the cabin site by himself, and with no assistance whatever built the entire cabin from floor to roof. Anyone aware of the arduous work with logs of such size will say it is not a one-man undertaking.

In 1885 a new road was built from Stanley to Barkerville, taking the place of the old one from Van Winkle around to Richfield and then down to Barkerville. This new road passed through a narrow, treacherous pass known as Devil's Canyon, which had to be vigilantly patrolled because of frequent snow slides. For many years Bill Brown was employed at this patrol task, which suited him down to the ground, as he was working by himself, and he had the added feeling of accomplishment, which he prized. By sheer strength and endeavor he kept the roads clear for travel. Often he was forced to shovel all night to have the pass open for the freight teams in the morning.

Bill had at one time worked on the drift mining at Lowhee. Years later when this section of the drift was being hydraulicked, a shovel bearing his initials was piped out. Russel MacDougall, who found and examined the shovel, identified it as undoubtedly Bill Brown's. On further examination it was found to be at least a quarter larger than any standard shovel used in drifting! Such was Bill Brown, compulsive worker—a rare breed in any age.

Brown's work in the Cariboo continued until the thirties. He died at Barkerville in January 1939. He had been born almost one hundred years earlier in December 1839.

Right up to a few years before his death he had continued to walk along the Lowhee tailings near the Jack of Clubs Lake, and with small spruce trees, stake out the winter road as a guide for the freight teams to follow. (Winter roads were established wherever possible as a protective alternative to the roads of summer. The roads were not plowed in those days. By spring they would be packed with compressed snow, manure and ice and took much longer to thaw than if not used.)

LESTER BONNER

Lester Bonner did a tremendous amount of exploration work in the district. He and his brother came to the Barkerville area in the early 1890s. He did a considerable amount of work in the Jack of Clubs area. But his principal development took place in Little Valley Creek, at a spot about three miles out of Barkerville, two hundred yards off the Bowron Lake Road.

Little Valley is broad and deeply drift-filled throughout. In 1902 L.A. Bonner formed a mining syndicate to do extensive testing in the valley. His West Canadian Deep Leads Company first put down many drill holes to bedrock in the hope of locating the gutter of the original channel. It then did considerable drifting and sinking of shafts. But though this work continued until 1913 Mr. Bonner was not successful in finding sufficient pay to justify further exploration. Nonetheless he held the property for many years with the hope of one day being able to continue.

In this exploration work many difficulties were encountered. One of the first pieces of heavy equipment installed was the boiler from Nason's original sawmill on Williams Creek. The thirty-six-horsepower boiler had been transferred to the Proserpine Mine some years before in order to run the four-stamp mill installed there. It was from here that Lester Bonner acquired it, hoping it would develop enough power to run the Cameron pumps and eighteen-inch Cornish pumps brought from La Fontaine Mine. However, he was forced to install two more eighty horsepower boilers, and in the end the great depth of the ground proved too much for the pumps. He had to run a two-hundred-and-fifty-foot tunnel from the bottom of the shaft and from this point a fourteen-foot shaft at last reached the bedrock.

Most of the expense of this venture, which was prodigious, was paid by British capital. Once when Mr. Bonner was describing this and other works, he was asked who in the world were his backers.

"Well," he said with a wry smile, "I see that you are a patron of one of them. You smoke Black Cat cigarettes, made by the Carraras people."

Other exploration work was done by Lester Bonner at Lightning Creek in 1919 and at the La Fontaine in the twenties. For some years he lived at the La Fontaine mine, and from here explored many of the tributaries of Lightning Creek. His last years spent in the Cariboo were on a placer lease held on Lightning Creek at Spruce Canyon, adjacent to the property where Fred Tregillus had been successful. For all his enthusiasm Lester Bonner did not attain the success that many others had, but his contribution to the area cannot be overlooked. He established valuable geological records with the tremendous amount of exploration work he did throughout the district. His efforts also contributed to the economy of the area. One of the small lakes enclosed within Wendle Park is named Bonner Lake in his honour.

DUNCAN MCINTYRE

Dunc McIntyre was a tradesman and carpenter who came into the area in the 1880s and knew a number of the first discoverers of gold. He was responsible for the building of many of the early water wheels on the creeks. His method of construction for these wheels was the mortise and tenon which method, of course, was applied to all construction of those days. He also acted as foreman of many placer operations, one of which was for the C.M. & S. Company on

California Gulch. He was well respected in the area and was a man of sound character and principles.

JAMES DUFFY

Jimmy Duffy, a packer in the late 1800s, later established one of the first farms on the Bowron River, where he grew hay and a variety of vegetables with considerable success. It was a small farm, so he had time to operate a good-sized trapline. Though he spent a rather isolated life in the wilderness he was by nature a genial man and a most interesting person to visit.

Jimmy recalled once an incident when he had caught a wily timber wolf he had been trying to trap for a long time. One day on checking his trap he saw that the wolf had finally been caught but had taken off with the toggle and trap. Jimmy, who that morning was without a rifle, followed the wolf's tracks, and a quarter of a mile away came upon him entangled in some willows. When asked how he could possibly have killed the wolf, he answered, "I had my stick with me and I teased him until he was really mad, then I threw my hat at him. He pounced upon my hat, and while he was thus engaged, I rapped him over the nose, stunning him. It was easy to kill him after that without any danger to myself."

The old Bowron River trail used to go right past his cabin and all travellers up and down the trail stopped to visit him. It was a welcome sight when snowshoeing up to Bowron Lake with a heavy load of furs on one's back to see the smoke curling from Jimmy Duffy's chimney on a cold, frosty evening. Jimmy always greeted the weary traveller with a royal welcome and immediately served up hot tea and food, talking continuously the while of interesting recent events and news.

ELMER ARMSTRONG

Elmer Armstrong spent many years prospecting on upper Grouse Creek, Antler and Proserpine Mountains. His interest was in the numerous quartz veins in these areas. He was finally successful during the thirties in selling his property on Proserpine to a mining company which did considerable exploration work on it. This was the New Proserpine Mines. This company later gave an option on the property to various other companies, but despite a great deal of work the veins on Proserpine have not as yet developed into a producing mine.

LEGISLATORS

Many of the early pioneers who came to Williams Creek served in the legislature. A few of these were: Dr. A.W.S. Black; Captain John Evans; Joshua Spencer Thompson; Joe Mason; I.B. Nason; F.S. Barnard; A.S. Rogers; Dr. M. Callahan; and Harry Jones.

14
FROM QUARTZ VEINS
TO QUARTZ MINES

The existence of quartz veins in and around Williams Creek and farther afield was known from the beginning of the placer discoveries. Gold-bearing quartz had been found in such places as Snowshoe Mountain, Red Gulch, Stouts Gulch and at the upper end of Williams Creek as well as on a mountain situated between Williams Creek and Grouse Creek, the Proserpine.

The Home Stake Company was greatly encouraged during the summer of 1866 by the promise of a Mr. McWorthy to have some of its findings assayed at San Francisco. He said that if it proved satisfactory, he would have a five-ton stamp mill brought up to work this ledge on Proserpine Mountain. However, nothing ever seemed to come out of this, nor of other quartz samples sent to San Francisco from numerous veins in the district. Whether or not the samples were lost in transit or what became of them the miners couldn't learn. All they knew was, of the large quantities of ore samples sent to that city very few reports, good or bad, ever were received by those anxiously awaiting the results.

The great necessity of a quartz mill to test the ore in the immediate vicinity prompted the mining board to approach the government asking its assistance in erecting such a mill. Meacham & Nason, owners of the sawmill at Richfield, pointed out to the government that their large water wheel was already established, and that they would gladly have it used for the proposed stamp mill. This was early in 1867. All pleas to the government failed, and at last a prospectus was prepared for the forming of a company to erect a quartz test mill. However, nothing seemed to come of this either.

It was not until October 8, 1877, that a government four-stamp mill was finally established at Richfield, and on that day began crushing ore at the site of Nason's sawmill.

After the year 1876 the output of gold from placer deposits in the district was decidedly falling off, and there was great eagerness on the part of miners and of everyone in the area to see a success made of an operating lode mine. Innumerable quartz veins were investigated. R.B. Harper, the government mining engineer, arrived at Williams Creek during the summer of 1877 and made an extensive examination of all the prospects. Eighty-four quartz mining claims were recorded after his arrival. The spirit of the entire population picked up. This was emphasized in the Minister of Mines Report of June 1877 in these words: "A year ago the miners of Cariboo, after long and patient struggling, had nearly given up hope; today everybody is looking forward to an era of prosperity which, in the opinion of the well-informed, will even exceed that of the palmy days of 1862-3-4-5."

The miners had never lost faith in the gold of the Cariboo. Their discouragement came rather from their long, unassisted struggle after the first quartz veins were discovered in 1863. A test mill had been so desperately needed. Also proper assaying of their finds was required before capital would be induced to invest in lode mining claims.

Although no one knew this at the time, it was yet to take many, many years of effort before the mines, which they were sure existed, were proved to be as rich as all confidently believed.

In those first years after 1877 there were most promising results from discoveries such as the Black Jack Ledge, situated at the south end of Barkerville. Early assays of this property were exceptionally good and in later years ran as high as $20 to $70 a ton. The Bonanza Ledge, between Lowhee and Stouts Gulch, assayed at $20 to $36 a ton. Some of the early assays of this ledge were later reported to be erroneous, and at that time the best assays were but $4 to $10 a ton. The assays from Proserpine Mountain Ledge showed no gold in some samples, and as high as 9.88 to 13.54 ounces per ton of gold in others. In the Island Mountain Ledge, three hundred feet above and overlooking Jack of Clubs Lake, five miles from Barkerville, early assays were not exceptional, being about $2 to $4 a ton, but faith in it persisted and brought it to success. The Rainbow Ledge on Cow Mountain, near Jack of Clubs Lake overlooking Lowhee Creek, was very rich in free, highly crystalline gold. Assays were good to exceptional. The Perkins and Beedy Ledges, two miles from Stanley on the southern slope of Burns Mountain, assayed at 2.6 ounces of gold to the ton with a high content of silver at 29.8 ounces to the ton. Six Mile Creek Ledge, on a tributary of Swift River, in early assays from San Francisco showed $125 to the ton in gold and silver. Incidentally, the fact that this assay return in 1876 came from San Francisco shows that evidently some returns did reach the Cariboo, even though so many did not. The source of this gold has been searched for by many people since the early days, but to date has not been discovered. Stedman's Ledge, on the right of Williams Creek just above the Richfield Courthouse, assayed at $18 to $20 a ton. In 1877 the lode from this ledge was believed to be a part of an immense fissure that extended from Grouse Creek to Red Gulch on Island Mountain. Interestingly enough, all the streams that crossed the lode were rich in placer deposits.

Although the assays on most of these properties showed such a high and encouraging gold content, the actual mining of the ore proved to be bitterly disappointing. An example of this was on the Black Jack Ledge. The mining company concerned put in a one-stamp mill on their ground and, after feeding ore which had assayed at $70 a ton, found the gold recovery amounted to only $18 to $20 a ton. It was evident that a very large loss was sustained in concentrating. This was true of all ore of that day. Science had not yet perfected a method of extracting all the gold from the sulphides. In the latter part of the century the Black Jack Company reported that $7,000 in gold had been recovered from the ore they had treated. This could easily have been trebled had the use of cyanide in gold recovery been known then and applied.

Cyanide had been used for gold recovery in South Africa in 1890, mostly on the tailings from amalgamation. It had been tried a year before this, in 1889, in New Zealand. However, the practice of using cyanide without previous amalgamation did not become widespread until 1925.

In 1888 the government built a reduction works at Barkerville about a mile north of town. It had a one-stamp mill and a cyanide plant. This did much to facilitate the recovery of gold from ore.

For all the efforts made by the miners in the last century, only two mines developed successfully and these did not come into completely successful operation until the 1930s. These two were the Island Mountain Mine and the one on Cow Mountain, developed by the

Cariboo Gold Quartz Mining Company. However, the gold from these two mines since then is far in excess of all the placer taken during the 1800s, and it fully justifies the early miners' firm belief in the quartz veins. Besides this there are at least three potential mines in the district, which are believed to be as rich as either of the two now in operation. The Black Jack, above Barkerville, is particularly rich.

The following brief account of the Island Mountain Mine's history gives some idea of the years of struggle and effort needed to bring a quartz vein to a producing mine.

The quartz veins of Island Mountain were first observed in 1863 near a small stream on this mountain called Red Gulch. In later years gold-bearing quartz was discovered not far from another stream, Mosquito Creek. Very little was done, aside from attempting to get assays, to develop these findings until 1876 when Samuel Walker took out some ore from his claim with the idea of discovering just how rich it might be. A couple of years later he sold his property to the Enterprise Company.

In the spring of 1878, this company employed a half dozen men to take ore from the claim, and in some three months had four hundred tons ready to haul to the mill. They had procured machinery for a ten-stamp mill from the BC Milling & Mining Company, who had not set up their projected twenty-ton stamp mill. With this equipment set up in an old shaft house on the Williams Creek Meadows—the Kurtz & Lane shaft house—they hoped to extract enough gold to warrant opening the existing veins and going into mining operations. This plan did not prove successful and although they carried on for two years, they were forced in 1881 to suspend operations.

By 1886 Peter C. Dunlavey had become the owner of the Island Mountain property. He was greatly heartened by a report of Koch and Craib, mining experts from California, describing better methods than those hitherto used in the district of reducing the ores for successful extraction of gold. A chlorinator or a concentrator was essential to success, their reports stated. The mining men of the district were appalled that men who had been placed in positions of trust as experienced in quartz had not seen fit to mention this in 1876 when the four-stamp mill was first built. Now with a concentrator in the offing Peter Dunlavey began mining with renewed vigor. He continued his tunnel far into the mountain, discovering as he went that the gold content of the ore improved with depth. By the next year he employed fifty to sixty men to remove the ten-stamp mill from the meadows to Jack of Clubs Lake, and to erect buildings and machinery at the lower end of the lake. Six men were taking ore from the mine.

By the year 1890 the Island Mountain Company had completed the ten-stamp mill and had attached an improved rock crusher and four concentrators. On August the 20th of that year the mill went into operation. Rock crushing began on September 25, and a month later several tons of ore had been pushed through. All looked promising that year and the company owners were optimistic. However, the same old difficulty of not being able to separate enough gold from the sulphides was met from the start. The resulting gold recovery was not encouraging, even though it was not considered to be a fair result, inasmuch as most of the ore had been taken from the dumps from various tunnels belonging to the company and was mostly surface rock. Through want of sufficient gold, recovery operations were suspended after a few years.

Many years later, in 1902, Seymour Baker, convinced that some better method of gold recovery would bring a quartz mine into operation, began work in that direction. He and his friend, Mr. Atkin, examined quartz properties throughout the district. They sank shafts, drove tunnels and pumped out the old workings on Lowhee Creek and on Burns Mountain. They leased the government Reduction Works, with its one-stamp mill and cyanide plant, and crushed and treated samples of ore ranging in amounts of one to fifteen tons.

The next year Baker went to England to get backing for his mining, and that year he and Atkins spent most of their time on Burns and Island Mountains, much of the work being done on the latter property. Here they were surprised to learn that although numerous tunnels had been drifted, some for a distance of three and four hundred feet, none had gone beyond a depth of fifty feet. The old-timers in the district reported that tellurides, which run up to 60 percent in gold content, had been found by early miners. At this time, after exhaustive tests, Baker and Atkins could find none, but in later years tellerium was found to exist in abundance both here and at Cow Mountain. (Later this was classified as bismuth.)

In this same year of 1903, Seymour Baker bought an old building which in early years had belonged to a Doctor Watt. In this he set up a complete assay plant and laboratory in Barkerville. His faith in finding a quartz mine never wavered, and from that year forth he examined and tested numerous quartz veins on Proserpine, Island, Burns and many other mountains including one on Tom Mountain about twenty miles from Barkerville. From this latter he installed a narrow gauge wagon road, over which he hauled the ore by team and wagon. The samples from Tom Mountain were highly promising. From Burns Mountain, on which J.C. Beedy of the early days had done extensive prospecting, the samples, too, were exceptionally good.

For the next thirty years Seymour Baker worked incessantly, taking samples of ore and treating them at his laboratory. He made many trips back to England to interest capital in the Cariboo mines.

Finally in 1933, after the success of the Cariboo Gold Quartz Mine at Cow Mountain, he was at last able to carry conviction that there was a potential mine at Island Mountain. He sold his mine to the powerful Newmont Company, who brought it into production. Shortly afterwards he left for England. This was reported to have been his fortieth crossing, and his first trip after a hard-won success. The word soon reached the district, however, that Seymour Baker had died on board the ship. Large payments for his property still continued to arrive in Barkerville. It seemed an ironical twist of fate that he did not live to enjoy fully the success he so richly deserved.

A similar struggle had gone on over the years with regard to the Rainbow Member on Cow Mountain before it was brought into production in 1932.

With its success, shortly followed by that of Island Mountain, the town of Wells, five miles out of Barkerville, was established. This became a flourishing centre with a population of over two thousand people and was the scene of another "rush" as the quartz boom of the thirties progressed.

The entire economy of the area was raised, as the early miners had so fervently believed it would be once a quartz mine was brought into production.

15
The Thirties

When I came to Barkerville in 1930 there was nothing at the present site of Wells, with the exception of the remnants of a few cabins, the Clark & McIntyre Sawmill building, built there in the 1890s, the log barn belonging to it, and the ruins of Seymour Baker's stamp mill. These were near the present site of the R. & H. Transport office.

For several years, Fred Wells had been prospecting in the area, near the southern slope of Lowhee Gulch on Cow Mountain, on what was known as the Saunders Vein. It had been discovered around 1882 and later opened up to some extent by Saunders who had put some of the ore through the reduction works with encouraging results. Fred Wells had prospected there for five years and finally got enough financial assistance from three Barkerville men, Tommy Blair, Tommy Nichol and George Turner, to enable him to drift into the mountain, which determined that the ore did go down in depth. This was sufficient encouragement for him to set up the Cariboo Gold Quartz Mining Company.

However, he was still not on the road, due to the fact that he couldn't get a favourable geological report. The geologists of that time maintained that ore could not exist to any depth in this formation, and without a report he was not permitted by the British Columbia Securities to sell shares in British Columbia.

As a consequence of this delay and frustration, in 1932 his directors, Dr. W.B. Burnett and O.H. Solibakke, who had great faith in Fred Wells and his property, took him to brokers in New York where he raised the additional needed money to put the Cariboo Gold Quartz mine into production.

In the winter of 1932–33, the townsite of Wells was being surveyed by Major Gooke of Quesnel, and the construction of many buildings was underway. Early in 1933 mining began and in the first year of production the output was $260,841. The mine had been operating continuously for over thirty years with a total output in excess of twenty-five million dollars. Fred Wells had been so disheartened and discouraged by geologists' statements on Cow Mountain prior to his success that for some years he refused to collaborate with them or acknowledge that any had been on his property.

By 1934 the population of Wells had reached the two thousand mark, supported by the Cariboo Gold Quartz and Island Mountain operations. All the building materials and equipment for the town and mine were hauled in by truck from Quesnel. A few buildings and homes were taken from Barkerville to Wells by Bill Balleaux on a snow road down the Meadows. As the houses passed the very doors of the old town's residents, Fred Tregillus, looking out from his porch, said, "They'll be bringing them all back to Barkerville some day." One of the houses moved was that of the lawyer, Hub King. He stayed in his office the whole way and remarked that he enjoyed the trip very much.

In 1934 when President Roosevelt pegged the price of gold at thirty-five dollars an ounce it was like a shot in the arm to all gold interests. This, coupled with the developments at Wells, brought dozens of mining companies into the area, and with them came men and machinery. Besides this, scores of prospectors came in on their own. The population of Barkerville swelled. New homes and businesses were built and new ventures started.

A few of the mining companies that arrived in Barkerville were the Amalgamated, Richfield, Newmont, Coronado, Cariboo King and Burns Mountain. These and numerous others did a tremendous amount of exploration and development work in and around the entire Barkerville and Stanley area, as far east as the Cariboo Hudson and as far south as the Cariboo Midas on the south end of Snowshoe Plateau.

At this time the population of Barkerville was about five or six hundred.

Until the early thirties there were few cars in Barkerville, perhaps no more than a half dozen. Joe House had one, and Dean Cochran, and a few others. Of course, the stage lines, of which at that time there were five, used large seven-passenger cars, usually Buicks. Even some of the freighters had only in recent years taken to trucks. Jack Campbell, one of the freight team drivers, continued using teams of six to eight horses and then retired just as the switchover was taking place.

Quite frequently supplies for various mining operations, lumber for flumes, etc., were still taken out in the winter on sleighs using horses.

The five stage lines, the BX, the I.T., the Houghtellings, the Cariboo and the Barkerville stage lines were in competition with each other for several years; finally, the Cariboo and Barkerville Stages remained. In the end the Barkerville Stage Line had the field.

Some of these stages, such as the BX and the I.T., ran thrice weekly from Ashcroft. Houghtellings ran daily from Prince George and Quesnel. Occasionally there would be a chartered stage from Vancouver.

It was an exciting thing to have these five stages arriving in Barkerville. Often they were filled with mining engineers, geologists and officials of the various mining companies as well as passengers still "bound for the gold fields."

Looking back on those days now, I think of the many wonderful people who lived there at that time. Many were descended from the first discoverers of gold. Others, like myself, had come into the old town in the early thirties.

The Rankin brothers were working at the Guyet Mine at this time. Their brother-in-law, Mr. Curtis, was managing it. They were the descendants of the Rankin who had staked one of the old, rich claims on Williams Creek in the early sixties. I used to snowshoe up to the Guyet in the winter days and visit them there where they stayed as caretakers during the off season, working during the hydraulic season. It was a pleasure to spend a weekend with these two who had such a vivid interest in the early mining days of Williams Creek and whose past had been linked with those pioneering times.

Elmer Armstrong died not long after selling his Proserpine property but his widow lived on for many years in Barkerville. I remember taking her up one day to Grouse Creek near the cabin where she had lived as a young woman. At the limestone dyke at the Waverly dam at Grouse Creek she said, "My goodness, how it has worn down! When I was a girl I used to step across this."

In January 1933, Lorna Boyd, who had been working in the government office at Quesnel was asked to come to Barkerville to help in the office there for a month. She remained for five years.

Lorna is a descendant of the original owners of the Cold Stream House and in speaking of this early Cariboo roadhouse she says, "My wonderful grandmother, Mrs. John Boyd, went to Cold Stream House as a bride of sixteen years. She brought with her six chickens from her home." (She had come from San Juan Island, Washington, where her sister lived.) She took them along, she said, so she would not be lonely or homesick! She had ten children of her own. When all were grown, the house was too quiet so she adopted an eleventh—a little girl.

Besides the people, many of whom have been introduced here in earlier pages, there were the nearby places where one might go to visit of an afternoon such as the Lowhee, Forest Rose, Richfield and the Waverly Mines.

The Waverly campsite, but four miles distant, was set in what can only be described as a natural park. There, an old-fashioned two-storey house stood in a grove of Aspen, through which ran a clear stream, supplying fresh, cold water. At a distance from the house were the outbuildings of the camp of 1879. These included Pat Carey's cabin, a stable and other small implement sheds.

Not far from the buildings a path leads one to the edge of the early Waverly pit. It is a breathtaking sight to come out of the woods and find oneself gazing down at this tremendous pit, which on second glance one observes slopes on down for a distance of a mile or so.

It was at Richfield that a link with the past was discovered by Dalby Morkill when he was surveying for one of the mining companies there. While making camp he came across a number of buried machetes, spurs, bits and bridles as well as a supply of nested copper mess pans. After considerable investigation it was determined that these items had belonged to the Royal Engineers who had been stationed at Richfield during the Grouse Creek War crisis. At that time, their warehouse containing equipment had mysteriously burned down, and all was buried in the ashes until Dalby found these, over sixty years later!

Another indirect link with the past came as a pleasant surprise to one Jens Hansen, who had been sniping for gold in some of the early pits. Sniping, it must be pointed out, is considered to be a worthy way of making wages. To go near another's sluice box or to snipe on someone's ground is a very grave offence and in the early days one might be shot if found near either. But when a claim has been abandoned, or if one has permission from the owner to do some prospecting on his property, that is a different matter entirely.

Jens had an uncanny knack of ferreting out the old wing boards of former workings and finding the gold left there. He managed to make a good living at it.

One time when he'd been particularly fortunate, he and a few of his cronies had been having a rousing good time from the proceeds at the Kelly Hotel bar, and for several days really whooped it up, when suddenly they ran out of money.

"Never mind, boys," said Jens, "we'll go out and get some more gold." They all trooped out, stopping to pick up pans and shovels on the way. They hadn't proceeded very far up Stouts Gulch, a favourite place of Hansen's, when he came across a really amazing find and called down, "O.K. boys, we've got it made. We can go back." They all stopped and awaited him and he showed them his find—a $500 nugget! In a mere hour after they had left they trooped back to the hotel with enough gold to assure them a solid week's carousing!

It is said that later on, Mrs. McKinnon asked, "Where is that lucky Swede?" This name he carried thereafter—the Lucky Swede.

There has always been a feeling of optimism and a sense of adventure in the very air of Barkerville, and this was as true then as at any time. There was never a lack of something to do nor inspiration to do it.

I remember one evening a few of us were sitting around chatting rather aimlessly. We were in a mood to have some fun and frolic and decided to go down to the old Theatre Royal and dance a bit. There were about six of us, and soon we felt that this just wasn't enough people. Then Ben said, "Come on, fellows. Just follow me." He had been playing his accordion at the time, and he started with it for the door. Ken Carpenter grabbed a gas lamp, and using this as a torch, they started up street, Ben playing "Men of Harlech."

As the rousing old Welsh song reached the ears of the people, doors opened, and heads popped out to see what was going on. Soon there was a small crowd following, and when they reached the Theatre Royal, Ben never hesitated but marched up the stairs and inside, playing as he went. Everyone followed and a successful evening of dancing ensued, remembered to this day by all who joined in.

The Labour Day weekend by long tradition was always a favourite celebrating time at Barkerville. These were three days of rollicking fun ending each evening in a dance. Horse racing was held on the long street, which was cleared of people for the purpose. The race started near the old Billy Barker shaft and proceeded to St. Saviour's Church. There might be only six or eight horses involved in the race, but this took none of the thrill out of it. Climbing a greasy pole for the prize of a bottle of liquor was another attraction. There were gold-panning contests, mucking contests, the usual broad jump and high jump and various forms of racing.

The highlight of each day's celebrations was the arrival of the stagecoach with passengers and mail. The stage was the last one of the original stagecoaches of the 1800s, and it was pulled by a four-horse team.

Bill Ward walked up and down the street with a megaphone announcing its progress. "The stage coach is nearing Jack of Clubs Lake. It's at McArthur's Gulch." Then finally he announced, "The stage is half a mile out of Barkerville." On its arrival a few "passengers" alighted, and the "mail" sacks were taken out. The "passengers" were dressed in old-fashioned clothes and were announced as well-known old-timers. At least once during the three days there would then be a "robbery" with the "bandit" chased, caught, tried and hanged.

On one of these occasions the ill-fated "bandit" was Howard Harris. He was duly chased, caught, put in leg irons and his hands tied behind him. Then the officiating members of the "hanging" put a noose around his neck and threw the rope over a T-bar and pulled him up, making sure his feet were always touching the ground. Just about that time a gang of roisterers, far gone in spirits, came booming along, momentarily scattering the "hangmen" and shouting, "Oh sure, hang him! Come on, let's hang him!"

Howard was of course rescued but he remarked afterwards that it was just a little too realistic for his liking. At times his feet had been barely touching the ground.

During the celebrations the town was wide open and there were many amusing incidents. There was the time when some of the boys grew tired of one of the group, who always after a few drinks became quarrelsome and started a brawl. "What shall we do with him?" they asked one another. Then one had a brilliant idea.

"Let's hang him up on the picket fence!" They picked him up bodily and hung him by his belt over the top of one of the pickets.

As he cursed them roundly, they quietly departed, leaving him suspended in the air, his feet off the ground and arms and legs dangling.

Labour Day at Barkerville, 1937. The prize for climbing the greasy pole was the bottle of whiskey seen tied near the top of it. Courtesy W.T. Ward

On another occasion a few celebrants were having a private party at "Uncle Dan's" cabin when a fellow they'd never seen appeared at the door. He staggered into the room much the worse for wear and the boys promptly ejected him. A few minutes later he reappeared. This time they gave him a double shot of whiskey and again pushed him out of the door, where he promptly passed out. Hours later they left for home and saw him lying there.

"Sure and we have a corpse on our hands," exclaimed Irish Anderson in mock dismay. "There's always a corpse on Labour Day."

"Let's bury him right here," exclaimed another. Thereupon they went for picks and shovels and were busy "measuring him up" when he came to.

He took one look at the shovels and picks, leaped to his feet crying, "You're not burying me!" and fled.

Bob Calder, one of the party, described it in one of his favourite expressions. "He fled like a bat out of hell, his coat pocket dipping dust as he rounded the turn at Hong's Store."

Hundreds of people attended the Labour Day celebrations. It was a time of wholesome outdoor fun and of reunion when long awaited friends might return for the occasion. All the chairs and benches on the verandahs of the hotels and stores were occupied, and the old-timers viewing the activities remarked how the old town had come to life.

These old-timers, many of whom were pioneers of the 1800s, had a hardiness of spirit that kept alive the adventurous early days. Their trails, camp sites, mines, cabins and homes were a visible part of the past and they themselves brought by-gone years into the living present.

16
RESTORATION

When war broke out in 1939 many people left to join the armed services or to take up wartime work. Gold mining suffered a severe setback and few of the lode mining companies remained in the Barkerville area. A few miners and prospectors still worked their small holdings, but only the best-established placer mining operations continued working. However, the general attitude was that after the war things would return to normal.

In early May 1945, I spent a week in Barkerville and staked some leases in the Quartz and Grouse Creek area. The possibilities of Grouse Creek still intrigued me as they had in the thirties.

We formed a small mining syndicate of twenty members and later transferred it to a private company. So in the fall of 1945, I returned once more, this time bringing with me my wife, Esther.

In 1946 we decided to remain in Barkerville just for one winter, but in fact for the next eighteen years Barkerville was to be our home.

There was enthusiasm and optimism in those first years after the war. Everyone felt confident that gold would make a comeback. As we know now, this did not happen. Gradually after five, then six, seven and eight years had passed and there was still no change in the gold picture, people began to lose some of that confidence. Gradually, too, first one and then another left Barkerville. Some went to Wells or Quesnel; others left the Cariboo entirely. Most of those who remained were still optimistic. But in time even they began to feel a change in the atmosphere and in the outlook.

Since we had arrived back in Barkerville, my early dreams of the thirties to preserve it as an historic site returned more strongly than ever. I had been stricken to learn that a few years before my return Seymour Baker's old assay office and workshop had been torn down. This building had originally belonged to Dr. Watt and was one of the structures built just after the fire. When Seymour Baker was there, it was a long, low building reaching almost to the back street.

It contained such priceless relics as his link chains, his old transit, a traverse wheel, a rock crusher and muffles, pulverizer and assay scales. All this equipment dated back to the 1880s, and most of it, of course, would be obsolete today.

In the late 1940s, other old buildings, considered a fire hazard, were torn down. For a while it seemed that every time we came into town from camp, we'd discover first another familiar building being razed and used for firewood or rebuilt somewhere else. I used to feel physically sick at this destruction, and even today the thought of it fills me with deep regret. We worked, at that time, long hours at the placer camp, and after the mining season we were usually away for some months, organizing the company for the next season and also working during the winter months. As a consequence, I was powerless to do anything to prevent the destruction of these historic buildings.

In the summer of 1947, the Government Assay office was torn down. This building dated back to the 1870s. In the thirties it was owned by Eldridge Metallurgists of Vancouver, who did work for the mines at Wells and also for many of the prospectors who came in with samples of ore. George Mailleau was the last assayer to work in this office, which was closed in 1934. The office had a long and varied history and was of inestimable worth historically.

That same year the old John Hopp office was torn down. This had been originally the Scott saloon, one of the very few buildings that had survived the 1868 fire at Barkerville. Destroyed along with it were boxes and trunks of old records, books and ledgers, precious souvenirs of early times.

Tommy Blair's store was the next to go. Peter C. Dunlavey, one of the first miners on Williams Creek, had once been a partner of the Blairs and had worked in this very store. It still had the long ladders running on tracks to reach the higher shelves and dozens of great wooden bins that had held bulk rice, beans, flour, etc.

When the old Hudson's Bay Post, rebuilt in 1868, and literally filled with ledgers, books and records which dated back to earliest times, was being torn down I longed to go up to Mrs. McKinnon to ask her if I might look through these records and keep any of value. But that old established custom of Barkerville, the hesitancy to concern oneself with a neighbour's affairs, prevented me from asking.

Besides these mentioned there were two or three Chinese dwellings and one Chinese business building torn down and used as firewood. These places were truly old, dating back to just after the fire. I wished at the time I could buy every old building in Barkerville and preserve it.

Tourists and souvenir hunters used to load their cars with chairs, tables, mirrors, books, letters and photos. They seemed to have no qualms and would find their way into any building that was not occupied. Where we, in Barkerville, would not have dreamed of entering a building just because its owner had left the town, even if he had gone years ago, they thought nothing of breaking a window to get in and of taking out whatever they wished. To them this was a ghost town. They looked on an untenanted house as just an old deserted building. We regarded it as the precious property of a one-time neighbour, well and personally known to us.

What with one thing and another I used to look at Barkerville and see it in the future failing, eventually falling to ruin, its history unknown and its story untold, and so I resolved to do something about it.

At that time, the people of Barkerville had formed the Barkerville Historic Society, and I was invited to join. I did eventually join the society, but I felt that to preserve Barkerville and the remaining buildings in it would be virtually a full-time occupation. It would require time and money—a good deal of both—and more than any volunteer society could ever expect to have. It needed organization and a long-term plan.

Later Quesnel formed the Cariboo Historic Society and asked various other towns to join. They were to be considered the parent society, each of the others donating a dollar per member, half of which would be for Quesnel, and half for the contributing society. Many towns, such as Williams Lake and Clinton, did not favour this plan, and in truth neither did Barkerville at first.

During the years since our return we had been collecting any items we could find from the early days and gradually had built up quite a sizable collection. Most of these were mining relics. However, some were not. We had, for example, an old still and also some candle lanterns and various other items of interest such as a box of wax matches donated by Gordon McArthur.

In 1952 I began formulating a plan to halt effectually the destruction of the few remaining buildings and to build Barkerville into a tourist attraction. I formed the Barkerville Historic and Development

Company, and early in 1953 our charter was granted. The company had three members, my brother-in-law, Ted Barnes, our lawyer, Mrs. McCrossan and myself. Our plan was to interest anyone with money to invest some in the development of Barkerville.

The few people in the town and in Wells and Quesnel who learned of our hopes and plans for Barkerville were skeptical. None thought our plan feasible; some felt that too much had already gone out of the town, and others frankly and honestly believed that preserving the history of the town was not worthwhile.

Nonetheless we ourselves were firmly confident. Furthermore, we had many friends and acquaintances who were enthusiastic, people who had visited the town and had been charmed with it and its many points of interest. A few had pledged financial support once we were underway.

Nothing should have stopped us, but something did. That something was lack of time. I was in those years still committed to my mining company. We had started certain developments which could not be left unfinished. We knew that we should put aside the mining and concentrate wholly on the new company, of which we had dreamed and talked for so long. But try as we might, we simply could not find the hours, the days and weeks necessary to make this a successful venture. Besides this, the few people in Vancouver with whom I discussed our developments in Barkerville said they could not see the point in developing old and dead history when there was so much progress yet to be made in new ventures. So, outside of those few who had already pledged support, no one showed any interest. And yet I knew that I could unfold a plan which would have interested the most skeptical. Indeed, it was intended that one day this must be done.

During all the years from 1947 on, I spoke to any government official I knew or could manage to see, about the great necessity of preserving Barkerville's history. I wrote letters and received answers. I spoke to newsmen and correspondents and to anyone anywhere who could in any way advertise our cause.

In April 1953, while the charter for our company was being processed, I went to see Mr. Thomas Sturgess, Deputy Minister of Trade and Industry, and told him of it and of the things we wished to accomplish. He was genuinely interested. "We've just been waiting for someone outside the government to draw Barkerville to our attention. This kind of thing has to come from outside, you know. Once you've started, Mr. Ludditt, you'll get all the support you need from this government, and I don't just mean moral support either," he said. It was most gratifying.

By the latter part of 1955 and early 1956 some of the fruits of our efforts were beginning to show up in the press. Now and again, someone would send me a clipping mentioning Barkerville and its historic possibilities.

During this time, too, Miss Bowron had been talking to various members of the legislature about the great necessity of restoring Barkerville. Ralph Chetwynd, BC Minister of Trade and Industry, showed a sincere interest and did a great deal in interesting other members of the House. It was his intention to seek a $10,000 annual grant for Barkerville in the house. This was in 1956. In fact, if any single member of government should get due credit for bringing the matter of Barkerville before the House, the name of Ralph Chetwynd must rank first. The sad fact that he passed away before his bill actually reached the legislature in no way takes this honour from him.

However, it should be pointed out here that had it not been for the many, many talks that Miss Bowron had with him and with the other members, and for my own efforts and talks to almost every department of the legislature and to the various writers of the press, the subject could not have been put before the House. I used to say to any in the government to whom I talked that regardless of what party was in, the one that put forth a bill making Barkerville an historic site would go down in the annals of history as the party that had done a far-sighted thing. It would be to its everlasting credit.

In the summer of 1955, we learned that the Governor General Vincent Massey was going to visit Barkerville on his tour of the province. The Wells Board of Trade took over the entire planning of this momentous occasion and brought it off most successfully. Every phase of the trip from Quesnel to Wells to Barkerville, the visit to the Cariboo Gold Quartz Mine where he was to see the pouring of a gold brick, the tour of Barkerville, the sights of the old town and the historic cemetery and the dinner in his honour to be held at the Wells Hotel, was decided upon down to the last detail.

In Barkerville Miss Bowron impressed upon us all the importance of this visit and said we were in fact meeting royalty, since he was the Queen's representative. When the Governor General arrived she had us all line up in front of the church where each was to be officially presented to him.

It is impossible to describe Miss Bowron exactly. She was lady-like in all her actions, truly dignified, and yet at the same time she had an irrepressible enthusiasm, inherited undoubtedly from her pioneering father and mother. This dual quality was never so evident as it was on this day of days. She was so dignified during this particular part of the visit. Yet a little later, after Mr. Massey had done his tour of the town and in fact was on his way down the street and leaving, she ran after him and called him back.

"Mr. Massey, you can't leave until you've seen Mr. Ludditt's museum," she called. Miss Bowron had known Vincent Massey in the Beaver Club, in London, and felt on almost a friendly footing with him. She insisted that he walk back and come in to look over my display. This he graciously did, and took an obviously real interest in it, expressing appreciation of the fact that someone had done something about preserving these relics.

It was during the little visit that he had with the people of Barkerville in front of the church that a coincidence occurred in which Nell Dowsett, the postmistress at Barkerville, and I were involved. I had procured a particularly nice gold nugget tie pin and wrote a few words saying that this was presented to him on behalf of the senior citizens of Barkerville. As soon as I presented it to him, he said, "I knew that someone would give me a piece of Barkerville gold." He immediately had his aide remove his own tie pin and put on mine.

At this precise moment, Nell Dowsett, who had also felt that a present should be given, was presenting his daughter-in-law, Mrs. Massey, with a set of gold nugget earrings. There had been no collaboration. Neither of us had any inkling that the other had even thought of a gift!

On March 27, 1956, word reached Barkerville that Mrs. McKinnon had died at Vancouver, where she had been ill and bedridden for over two years. To us, it was as if the first lady of the land had passed away. We couldn't mourn, knowing how very much she and her family had suffered through her illness. It was, however, the sad end of an era, and was marked as such in our hearts.

At the end of 1956, George Kelly closed the store that had been left to him and his sister Mabel. This was the end of nearly a hundred years of mercantile trade in Barkerville. In 1957 he began plans to

St. Saviour's Church, Barkerville.

make a museum, but first he asked me if I minded or had intended to do the same thing. I assured him that I not only didn't mind but was very much pleased that he was going to do something with the many items of the past that were in his possession. Often in the past I had tried to impress on him the historic value of the hundreds of items that were in the Kelly and McKinnon sheds and attics, more than enough to create a museum of distinction. Every article he showed me was to my mind of priceless value historically. I remember one in particular, the lamp that in the last century had hung outside the old

The interior of St. Saviour's Church. Courtesy *Prince George Citizen*

Kelly Hotel, on which was written, "Kelly Saloon and Beds." George opened his museum in 1957. It was an immediate success.

Although the Governor General's visit had done quite a lot to focus attention on Barkerville, still the months went by, and the new year of 1957 began, and still there was no word or sign from the government as to whether or not anything was going to be done. The province's centennial was the next year, and it seemed that if anything were to be accomplished it should certainly be at this time.

It was getting late and almost past the time when the BC Centennial Committee had to be notified by any communities that they intended to participate in the Centennial project. If intentions weren't in by a certain date the government would give no financial assistance to such projects. I made a number of enquiries around Wells and Barkerville to see if anyone had intended to suggest a project, and finding that none had, I wrote to Mr. L.J. Wallace, Chairman, BC Centennial Committee, Victoria.

His answer, and other letters that followed, convinced me that nothing had so far been done by anyone to date. However, it also clearly showed that though we were late, there was yet time to begin a Centennial project.

Following correspondence with Victoria we formed the Wells-Barkerville Centennial Committee. Except for myself, all the members of this committee were from Wells, and each one of them put forth great effort, without which it would not have turned out to be the success it was. The members were: Angus MacLean; Ross McIvor; Mr. and Mrs. James Forman; and Nelson Brown. Barney Green, Mrs. Paul Peche, Tim Coleman and Russel MacDougall were on the sub-committees.

We discussed various possible projects for the Centennial. I suggested the writing of a small history of the Cariboo and volunteered to do this on my own. The idea was to write a brief item about some of the better-known claims of the sixties, then by numbering the claims to correspond to the booklet and by erecting small sign boards we could facilitate the easy locating of them by the tourists. This project was adopted, and I set about to compile the small booklet, *Gold in the Cariboo.*

When the articles were finally compiled, Bob Green, the school principal at Wells, agreed to edit it. Though hard-pressed for time, he willingly and even happily began this task. His wife, Pat, retyped each article.

The project was a success. We set the price at only fifty cents a copy, and by the end of the Centennial Year we had sold just under three thousand; by October 1959, we were able to pay our share of the cost of printing, put two hundred dollars into the Wells Ski Hill and place over four hundred dollars and some three thousand of the books into the hands of the local historical society.

During 1957 so much attention was being focussed on Barkerville that suddenly there seemed to be too many visitors. Almost every week someone came up to Barkerville to get information for articles or to ask questions and to volunteer suggestions about things that we had discussed and planned years before. It all seemed very ironical to me in view of the apathy displayed in earlier years when I had been trying so hard to get support from anyone who would listen.

George Kelly had one or two offers for his museum. Some wanted the exhibits, as they were going to build a museum in their own town and would have a "Barkerville Room" in which his articles would be placed. One offer was from the United States. George would rather have crated every item and stored it than have had it taken out of Barkerville.

During this same year, 1957, William Speare, who had succeeded Ralph Chetwynd as Cariboo member, noting that, despite all the talk of what was going to be done by the government, so far exactly nothing had been accomplished, decided to pick up from where Mr. Chetwynd had left off. He asked Ross McIvor, Angus MacLean and me if we would prepare a brief for him to present to the legislature. This we did.

In the brief we outlined our reasons for believing that Barkerville should be declared an historic site. We mentioned the large numbers of tourists that came each year and had been coming for years; and suggested that facilities should be made available for these tourists. We also pointed out that many of the original buildings had already been torn down and the few remaining were threatened, and that if nothing were done soon the town would be lost to history. We mentioned that there was now a privately owned museum in the town which could be a good beginning for any future work done by the government. In November of that year Mr. Speare was at last to come up and look over our brief.

The reference in our submission to the remaining buildings was indeed the truth. That very fall I happened to meet a couple of the bachelors coming down the street dragging a hand sleigh and some old logs and asked them what in the world they were doing. They replied that they had been given permission to tear down two old Chinese log buildings on the back street and also the original Moses Barber Shop building. As there were very few original buildings left my heart leaped.

"Don't go any further with it," I said. "I'll take the responsibility for them not being torn down." Thus, by a mere chance these buildings were saved.

Despite the brief, the weeks wore on and November was nearly over and still there was no concrete evidence or word of any action being taken. Then who should unexpectedly appear at Barkerville but two members of the editorial staff of the Prince George *Citizen!* These young men spent the best part of two days in the town taking photographs of and interviewing the citizens of Barkerville. They dedicated one complete issue of their paper to write-ups and photographs and emphasized the historic value of this town in superb editorials. After the paper was published, they sent us several dozens of copies for distribution. They argued well for the restoration of Barkerville.

In the spring of 1958, I went over to Victoria and asked at the parliament buildings if there were any plans to do something about preserving Barkerville and for establishing facilities to accommodate the hundreds of tourists we expected to visit the old town in the Centennial Year. Their reply was negative.

On June 19, 1958, I received a wire from the BC Dept. of Recreation and Conservation asking me if I would take temporary charge of the restoration of Barkerville. To this I agreed. I was instructed to hire four or five men to help with the project. I picked out four who seemed to me to be the best of all possible people to do this work. When they agreed to help, we began at once to restore first the barbershop and the Chinese buildings on the back lane.

At last the restoration of Barkerville had truly begun! It seemed almost a miracle that my dream was materializing. C.P. (Ches) Lyons, well-known author of many books on British Columbia, was on the Provincial Parks Branch and in a supervisory position. He came up frequently and looked over the town, jotting down notes and plans of what was to be done.

One of the first and most important things was to provide a suitable camp site with tables, restrooms and cooking facilities. Very shortly these arrived and were erected as quickly as possible since July 1 was the deadline.

We worked, too, that first summer on the old cemetery. Some of the headboards were so ancient the inscription had sunk out of sight into the board. The task was to reconstruct the wording. In many ways it was a rewarding experience. There was a definite feeling of accomplishment to be able gradually to make out the ancient lettering by turning the board in this or that different light. Many of the headboards had inscriptions in Welsh, which further complicated the task.

It was while this work was going on that there was widespread comment about the missing headboard of Chartres Brew, which had been taken from the cemetery by the Cariboo Historical Society as a prank and to draw attention to themselves. Many of the tourists asked where the headboard was. They had seen its photographic reproduction in *Gold in the Cariboo* and were most interested in it. This couldn't have happened at a more awkward time for us, and it certainly didn't help our cause to have to tell them that it had been stolen from the cemetery. It was finally found, stored in a shed in Quesnel, and later returned to the Parks Branch.

However, in restoring this headboard, instead of using the same rustic wood and methods by which it had been originally constructed, the Parks Branch chose to use several layers of laminated plywood! Many of the tourists have commented to me about this and asked why such an obviously artificial piece of work should be found in an historic cemetery.

As the weeks and months progressed, there were some things that the Parks Branch did with regard to this reconstruction of Barkerville which did not meet with our wholehearted approval.

As it was, there was no liaison between the old residents of Barkerville and those actually doing the restoration. The advisory committee in Victoria was composed of fine and able men. They had recommended that a local committee consisting of residents and pioneers be set up so that their knowledge and that of others from the past could be an assistance to project directors. Regrettably, this was not done. The local branch of the Historical Society was taken over and run by employees of the Parks Branch with its main function centred at Barkerville. It might better have been kept separate and operated on a wider range so that authentic historical information of the area surrounding the park could have been made available by its own residents.

In illustration of what this lack of liaison produced, we may take the case of one of Billy Barker's shafts, which then was still in existence. The original collar of this two-compartment shaft and some of the logs were visible. The author and others suggested that a replica of the shaft house could be built on this actual foundation. The integrity of this restoration would have been that much more obvious. Instead of this, the collar and logs were buried, obliterating all evidence that a shaft had ever existed. The *material used was crushed rocks from the Shamrock dump,* not even authentic-looking waterworn rock and gravel from the adjacent stream bed. On top of this new fill a small crib frame was put in and a windlass and shelter built above it. The improbable result, which any miner would recognize as a poor imitation in lieu of what had been available as the real thing now is depicted as Billy Barker's shaft! A valuable object of history, in effect, was destroyed in favour of a poor and patently unsuitable substitute.

When one looks at the overall picture of the park development such discrepancies may seem of small moment, and perhaps in total perspective they are, but they caused residents, including the author, a good deal of unhappiness at the time. It would have been so easy then to have done better. Yet there are many things of genuine authenticity that do much to offset these feelings of disappointment and create in the visitor a feeling of having stepped behind the curtain of time back into the surroundings and sights of more than a century ago.

17
IN TRIBUTE TO THE PIONEERS

Through this story of a gold camp, I have tried to record the authentic account of the work and life of some of the most important pioneers and of their descendants who maintained that optimistic spirit which lent a stabilizing influence over the area for three generations and until the historic park was established. Many of the very influential men and women of British Columbia at one time lived in the goldfields of the Cariboo where they made their first fortunes, then used their wealth constructively elsewhere in the new colony and province. Both those who left and those who remained in the Cariboo contributed something of lasting value to British Columbia. They should not pass into history unrecorded.

In many ways the park at Barkerville is a tribute to our pioneers, for in its museum are references to many of them. It will require further time and work to complete, under the government's long-term plans, but as it stands it is an impressive sight. The signs seen as one enters and the big water wheels are in good taste and appropriate to the surrounding country and the purpose of the historic site. The large, working water wheel farther up at Williams Creek is a stirring reminder of the past.

There are, too, hundreds of items from the past that bring to life the bustling days of the golden sixties. These are treasures some of us had thought never to see here again. But they have been well collected for posterity to see.

The wax images in the various buildings are life-like enough to have startled many a visitor. The replicas of the old buildings themselves represent tedious hours of research. They are stained in such a manner as to make them appear old, but somehow they still seem new and fresh, as one can imagine they must have looked to the inhabitants of Barkerville in those exciting years of the Cariboo Gold Rush.

In the tourist travel season the Barkerville Show, as presented by a troupe of entertainers from Vancouver, performs twice daily

Fred and Esther Ludditt at Barkerville's Cornish Wheel, 1971. Courtesy Michael Weiss

to full houses. This show has now become so well known that after the season closes at Barkerville it has engagements throughout the province and in 1967 travelled across Canada and appeared daily at Expo 67 in Montreal. A long-play recording of music from the show sells at Barkerville and elsewhere as a souvenir and an effectual advertisement for the park.

In order to appreciate fully what the park holds for the visitor, he should be prepared to spend at least two days or more, to observe and study at his leisure the many articles on display in the restored buildings, and to take part in such activities as gold panning and stagecoach riding.

The park has other values, too. Future generations visiting it will learn of the Cariboo Gold Rush and the tremendous part it played in the development of the vast interior of British Columbia and of Western Canada. It is a great satisfaction to know that the government has seen fit to take on another "first" project—the restoration of what was at its heyday the largest "city" in western America west of Chicago and north of San Francisco.

Of the one hundred thousand visitors who go through the park each season some are former residents returning to their old stomping grounds. Most are tourists from all parts of British Columbia, Canada, United States and Great Britain. They see Barkerville as it was in the 1860s. But somehow the residents see it, too, as it was long after the gold rush was over. They catch fleeting memories of bright, gay days, former days, when there was the excitement of still fabulous clean-ups, Labour Day celebrations or just the prospect of a lively dance in the old Theatre Royal. It is all there, in the park, memories from a past that is over one hundred years old.

But there are memories of Barkerville only a book can contain and preserve. The collection of stories here recorded has been a labour of love. The writer met and talked with these pioneers, heard their stories at first hand and committed them to note form against the day when a book could be developed. He lived amongst the sons and daughters of the pioneers who had made their lives in the Cariboo, calling it home and preferring its frontier life to any allurements the softer ways of big city life might offer. He saw the revival of hard-rock gold mining days when the town came to life again and participated in the further developments that have brought the Cariboo economically into modern times.

For many years it appeared that this remote and colourful cradle of Western Canadian culture in isolated Williams Creek would disappear by ransacking and deterioration. This would have been a reproach to all of us who should see in history the basis of a people's pride and appreciation of their heritage. To have had a part, with others who were like minded, in this preservation and restoration and to see, now, that far into the future succeeding generations will have a glimpse into the life of the first White men to follow the fur traders, is a gratifying reward for any labours involved. Equally, however, it has been a deep satisfaction to have made the human contacts with a people, and a way of living and of thinking, that were open-hearted, friendly, helpful and forever optimistic. In the nature of the qualities always called for in those who must push back the reluctant frontiers of Nature in a rugged country like Canada, there exist many of the attributes we can hope will persist among our young people. If this hope is well-founded, its fulfilment will much depend upon a widespread understanding of who and what the pioneers were, and how they made their contribution to the making of British Columbia.

Index

Page numbers in **bold** refer to images.

ABOUT THE AUTHOR

When Alfred William Ludditt came to Canada at an early age from his birthplace in Birmingham, England, his stonemason father located in Regina and travelled over much of Saskatchewan at his trade. His son was to be interested in rock not for its building qualities but for what it would yield in minerals.

In 1927 Fred Ludditt moved to the Kootenays in British Columbia and prospected for some years in mining districts around Nelson. In 1930 he made his first contact with the famed Cariboo gold area, where he placer mined on the Fraser and Quesnel Rivers. He settled in the historic Barkerville camp and lived there until 1937. While mining and exploring in that region he became a student of old records and reports in search of leads for placering or lode mining ground. He read what he could find, printed or hand-written, and talked with old-timers of the mining game in the area. Out of this grew a fascination with the almost literally unwritten history of the country. His research notebooks through the years began to comprise a history vital with the words and the personalities of many of the men who, as youths, had been in touch with old Cariboo days and with the almost legendary figures of the gold rush.

There followed for Ludditt a five-year interlude in mining at the Zeballos camp on the West Coast of Vancouver Island, but when that was done, he returned to Barkerville with a feeling that this was his chosen and spiritual home. Then he began in earnest his often-discouraging campaign to save Barkerville as an historic site and to leave for posterity in book form this unique record of Barkerville days.

Karin Ludditt, Fred's daughter writes: "My father lived to be eighty years old and was pleased to see me get married and have my first son in 1987. He died a few months later from lung issues brought on by years of smoking as well as breathing creosote and coal smoke from our home fires in Barkerville and Wells.

"It was a beautiful summer day in August, and my brother Frankie and I stood beside his hospital bed. I placed my son, then one-and-a-half years old, next to him, and though he had slipped into a coma, we knew Dad was aware, as he stroked the baby's knee. It was peaceful and quiet when he passed. He didn't get to die in Peru where he had worked in the Andes or in a cabin at Grouse Creek, but his children and a new grandchild were with him in the end."